There's An Adult In My Soup

There's An Adult In My Soup

Kim & Jason Kotecki
illustrated by **Jason Kotecki**

JBiRD iNK, Ltd.
109 Knutson Dr. Madison, WI 53704
www.jbirdink.com or 608-554-0803

This book may be purchased for educational, business, or sales promo-
tional use. Quantity discounts available.

Printed in the United States of America.

First Paperback Edition

Library of Congress Control Number: 2009930287

Publisher's Cataloging-In-Publication Data
(Prepared by The Donohue Group, Inc.)

Kotecki, Kim.

   There's an adult in my soup / Kim & Jason Kotecki ; illustrated by
Jason Kotecki. -- 1st paperback ed.

   p. : ill. ; cm.

   Includes bibliographical references.
   ISBN-13: 978-0-9715253-6-8
   ISBN-10: 0-9715253-6-6

1. Stress management. 2. Stress (Psychology)--Prevention. 3. Self-help
techniques. 4. Self-actualization (Psychology) 5. Inner child. I. Kotecki, Jason W. II. Title.

RA785 .K6 2009
155.9/042   2009930287

For our grandparents,
who paved the way for us with
integrity, hard work, sacrifice,
and faith.

When I was a kid, my soup was just right,
Yummy and tasty, a veritable delight.
Two cups of dreams and a full pint of play,
A pinch of curiosity for the perfect bouquet.
Passion and wonder and faith it had too,
I'd dare you to taste a happier stew!

But when I got older, my soup it did turn,
Enough to warrant a cause for concern.
It's gunky and goopy and lacking in fun,
It's not nearly as tasty as when I'd begun.
It's bland and it's bitter and tastes just like poop,
The problem is clearly the adult in my soup!

Are Grown-Ups Obsolete?

by Jason

You might think my answer to that inquiry would be an obvious and resounding yes. A friend sent me a photo of some sidewalk art he saw in London depicting a little girl holding a sign that says, "Grown-ups are obsolete." I love it. And it caused me to seriously consider the question: are grown-ups obsolete?

I hesitate to say yes, for fear that it would discount the wisdom of our elders. Fresh off a trip to San Diego for the National Speaker's Convention, I am torn. As important as it is to have the energy and optimism of youth, the wisdom and experience of life's veterans are just as crucial. Some of the best role models I see in the speaking profession—and in all walks of life—are the ones who actually had the opportunity to vote for or against Jimmy Carter. (And if you don't know who he is, you're obsolete.) They've been through many of the ups and downs of life; they are living road maps, alerting us to the potholes and steering us to the highways that lead to happiness.

So you can see my conundrum. Casting these people aside by labeling them as "obsolete" simply because of their age seems awfully rash. But then I thought of how my friend Michael Scott Karpovich defines a grown-up.

"A grown-up," he says, "is someone who is done growing."

Now *that* makes a lot of sense. Kids are growing all the time, physically and intellectually. They can't help it. Change is constant. There is always something new to learn and experience. But something happens to many people when they graduate from school (high school, college, grad school, you name it). It's as if they see that piece of paper called a diploma as an official proclamation stating, "Congratulations! You did it! You've learned all there is to learn; you have all the knowledge you need to make a go of it! Your training is complete."

> A grown-up is someone who is done growing.

Sounds a little silly, but it's the truth, isn't it? We as

a species don't particularly like change. While we're in school, there's not much we can do to avoid it. But once we're out on our own, it's easier to resist change. We settle into habits. We stop exploring. We stop asking questions. We don't push ourselves. We've become grown-ups.

And we become obsolete.

The role models I spoke of earlier are not obsolete. Because they're not really grown-ups. They continue to challenge themselves, to ask questions, to learn, and to grow. If you don't want to become obsolete and left in the dust, that's what you have to do, too. Because as fellow professional speaker Daniel Burrus says, "Everything that grows changes, and everything that changes grows."

Unless you're a grown-up.

Busy: The New Four-Letter Word

by Kim

Everyone is busy. Enough already.

Do you find yourself unknowingly getting thrown into the "busyness" contest? Whether it's at work or with family or acquaintances, people start talking about how busy they are. Before you know it, you too are spouting about how little time you have. For some reason, it seems like the busiest person wins. What a twisted and damaging conversation!

I am officially making "busy" a bad word, in order to avoid the trap of not only the aforementioned conversation, but mostly the mentality. It's poisonous. The funny thing is that everyone has the same amount of time, so if you are "busy," it's your own fault. The flaw is in you.

The other day we got a comment from someone unsubscribing from the K&J Insider, our free e-newsletter. Since we are always looking for ways to improve it, after someone unsubscribes there is a comment box, which is not a required field. It says, "We care what you think. Please give us your feedback on the Kim & Jason Insider so we can make it better for everyone. Thanks!" This particular unsubscriber chose to take the time to comment, sharing, "I didn't really want to spend time explaining why I am asking you to take me off the list. Time is what I don't have. It's a great site, just not interested anymore."

Ironically, she spent even more time telling me that she doesn't have any time. How funny! The line that struck me is, "Time is what I don't have." People love to be martyrs about their time.

Admit that you do have enough time. So much of it, that you don't have to be so busy. It's all about the little choices you make every day, your time management, and your priorities. It all comes back to you.

Has the modern culture's obsession with the "I'm so busy" mantra turned into a crutch that enables you to avoid taking 100% responsibility for your life?

It's time to stop talking about how "busy" you are and start doing something about it.

When Mosquitoes Attack
by Jason

The other night Kim and I were on one of our walks. It was late, and our steps were guided by the full moon's glow and the occasional street light. We were immersed in a great conversation brainstorming about the business. As we passed a park, my wife, who has a bladder the size of a baby leprechaun, spotted a port-a-potty. She had to go.

Did I mention it was dark? Ink black dark.

My role as husband meant that I was enlisted to hold the door open for her so she could see what she was doing. (Although in my experience, the less I'm able to see in those things, the better.)

No problem, I was happy to oblige. Except for one thing: over the past several weeks, Mother Nature had given Wisconsin enough rain to be declared a national waterpark. And with lots of rain come lots of mosquitoes, (a.k.a the Wisconsin State Bird.) The bugs don't really bother us on our walks, as long as we keep walking. If you stop to tie your shoe, or say, go to the bathroom in a darkened portable toilet stationed in the middle of a dark field blanketed in wet grass that hasn't been cut in ages, you're in trouble. Those pesky pests swarm around you like they're Homer Simpson and you're a donut with sprinkles.

So here's the picture for you: Kim was in the bathroom, trying to do her business as fast as she could. I was holding the door open while simultaneously trying to keep myself in mosquito-averting motion, pacing back and forth like a nervous expectant father on WAY too much caffeine. And the kicker is that, right in the middle of the whole ordeal, a car drove by. I'm not sure if their bright headlights allowed them to see what was going on, but I'd sure love to know what they were thinking.

We could all use more humility, but I've found that we don't usually have to seek it out. Never forget that you can spend most of your day acting like you're hot stuff; but whether you're a highly-paid CEO, a high-court judge, or just a guy out walking with his wife, life has a way of making sure you don't take yourself too seriously.

18 Checks
by Jason

I was chatting over email with my uncle recently, and the subject of following one's dreams came up. He expressed how sad it is that so many people wait until they retire before they pursue their dreams and goals. Unfortunately he noted, for many, that day never comes. This is from a guy in his mid-fifties coming off a quadruple bypass operation.

He mentioned that when people retire, the average number of Social Security checks they are able to cash before they die is...eighteen. I'm not sure what his source is, but I have no reason to question this number.

To me, life is too short to spend it living for retirement and 18 checks.

Now mind you, I am writing this from the cool confines of the Atlanta Bread Company because it is so hot here in Madison that I think I heard the weatherman say something about spontaneous combustion, and Kim and I are too poor to run our terribly inefficient air conditioner. In short, chasing after "the dream" is not always a picnic in Paris. Actually, on some days, it can be terrifying, frustrating, and can even make you question your sanity. But even though it's sometimes hard to explain why, I wouldn't change a thing. Not for a million dollars. Not for free air conditioning.

And definitely not for 18 checks.

FTERA. Do You Have It?

by Kim

I have been given much good fortune in my life, but little compares to the blessing of my in-laws. Jason and I are constantly acknowledging how grateful we are for the excellent role models we have in our parents. I got an email from my father-in-law the other day, who just happens to be one of the wisest people I know. He has identified a condition that often accompanies Adultitis, which he called FTERA (Failure To Enjoy Recent Accomplishments).

Do you have this condition?

It's what happens when we do not take time to delight in the little things and maintain perspective. Society tells us that we are not content. We need more. We need the next new thing in order to be happy. This causes us to be in a state of constant conflict and worry. When do we ever get to enjoy the successes of today?

I know that in business, as soon as you launch what you've been working on, you take a quick breath, then almost instantly feel like someone is out there doing what you just tried to do...*only better.*

This problem comes up often in families as well. As soon as Junior has made it through the soccer season, there is restlessness and discontent until the next thing is happening.

You finally get that raise at work that you've been stressing over, and the next day you move on to the next problem to worry about.

My father-in-law has outlined some ideas for a cure to this condition.

First, come to the realization that you can't handle everything out there. There is just too much of everything. So get that straight in your head first. Society is telling us what we want; but what we don't realize is that, if only we looked inside, we would find what we really want.

Second, visualize going to a great buffet. It all looks good; but if we ate everything, we would burst. Pick and choose what you really, really like and enjoy it! Pattern your life that way. Pick what you like, do it the best you can, enjoy what you accomplish. You know, take a deep breath and just enjoy it and then move on to the next thing.

Life is overwhelming. As soon as we think we are in control, we are in trouble. Delight in the joys of today for we don't know how many tomorrows we will have.

While You Were Busy, Life Passed By

by Jason

Last week, I enjoyed a nice vacation in Door County with the fam. We rented a house that was just big enough for the eleven of us: Mom, Dad, my brothers' families, Kim and me. We roasted marshmallows, fished for salmon, gazed at the stars, played mini golf, sampled wine, sat on the beach, and ate lots of cherry-related products (thumbs up on the cherry barbecue sauce). I also did something I haven't done in years: I didn't check email or surf the internet once.

Somehow, the world continued to rotate on its 23.5-degree axis.

Now, it took some planning and preparation to pull

it off. I cleaned up my email inbox, prepped all the web site files, and trained my colleague Jenna to do the updating. I had intended to check email mid-week, but once I got a taste of living low tech, that goal didn't take long to evaporate. It was a relaxing week.

And now for emphasis: the sun still rose and set on a regular basis and the business didn't crumble to the ground.

Hmphf. It all makes me wonder why I place such a high degree of urgency and importance on checking my email so many times a day. There were plenty of internet cafés I could've visited to "stay connected." (Or in other words, "stay distracted.") But then I might have missed out on playing catch with my brother, talking about our hopes and dreams. I might have missed out on the spirited game of Disney® Uno with my nieces. Or the refreshing walk with my bride amidst a green cathedral of pine trees.

Our world is connected like never before. And all of our technological advancements are supposed to give us more time. Instead, we fall for the temptation of trying to pack more tasks into the time we've saved.

I heard a saying once that if the devil can't make you bad, he'll make you busy.

Adultitis thrives in all this busyness. And all this busyness tricks us into feeling like we're productive. When we feel productive, we think we're actually getting something accomplished. And when we think we're getting something accomplished, we are fooled into believing that our work is not only obligatory, but indispensable.

Here's what's really happening: life is passing us by.

We miss out on the important stuff because we're convinced that the busyness is standard operating procedure. And we're deceived by the mirage that someday, if we work hard enough, our to-do list will be cleared. As David Allen reminds us in *Getting Things Done*, you will die with things STILL on your to-do list.

This never-ending hamster wheel is the part of adulthood we need to escape from now and then. As difficult as it may seem, we need to unplug ourselves from the daily grind. To think it's not possible is not only wrong, it's flat out foolish. If your situation is really bad (like checking-your-cell-phone-for-messages-every-minute-on-the-minute bad), perhaps you should consider an all-out "tech sabbatical."

These are the questions you need to seriously ask yourself: Do you really need to work extra to afford that latest gadget? Will life cease to exist if you don't check your email three times before breakfast? What's the worst that will happen if you don't answer your cell phone while you're having lunch with a friend?

Can you detach yourself from busyness for an hour a day? A day a week? A week every three months?

Here's the biggie: What will you miss if you don't?

Trading the Cracker Jack Prizes for the Peanuts

by Jason

What good is life if you can't slow down long enough to enjoy it once in a while?

Kim and I had a fortunate opportunity come our way last Friday night. We spent the bulk of the day downtown at a café with our laptops open, writing, thinking, and dreaming. As we packed up to go home, a young woman (and fellow Mac user) sitting nearby offered us two free tickets to the Madison Symphony Orchestra. The face value was over sixty bucks each. She told us she wasn't able to use them and was hoping to find someone who could.

What the heck, we thought.

A few hours later, I found myself sitting in Madison's new Overture Center, all spruced up and ready for some culture.

I am sure that the full magnificence of the performance was somewhat lost on me. But I can certainly say that it was wonderful to watch people who are really good at what they do, even if I don't know the difference between a viola and a cello. A world-renowned pianist was a featured guest. He had a bucketful of prestigious awards that I had never heard of, and yet even I could tell that he didn't just play music, he *lived* it. It was a part of him.

It was nice to sit there and take it all in. To relax, just letting the music stir my soul and refresh my spirit. I am grateful for the generosity of that nice Mac girl, whose name I never did get.

Later that night, I stumbled upon the report of a little experiment that *The Washington Post* recently conducted. They wanted to know what would happen if a world-famous classical musician played, not in a concert hall, but in a Washington D.C. train station, in the middle of morning rush hour. Would people know who he was? Would they at least realize that he wasn't your average street musician, and take a few moments to take in the free concert? Would they marvel at his $3.5 million Stradivarius? And exactly how long would it take for his violin case to be filled up with tens and twentys?

The musician *The Post* tapped for the experiment was a man named Joshua Bell, a 39-year old, critically acclaimed virtuoso. Ironically, I had heard of Joshua Bell for the first time in my life just hours earlier; it was announced he'd be playing a one-night-only performance in Madison at the Overture Center.

For a little less than an hour, Bell played some of the most difficult and other-worldly musical pieces known to man. Almost 1,100 people walked by.

Only seven people stopped, at least for a minute. Twenty-seven gave money as they walked by—some just pennies—for a total of $32.17.

1,070 of the people passed without giving the performer even a quick glance.

The Washington Post interviewed people after they passed by. One man, Calvin Myint, walked within four feet of Bell, and didn't have so much as a memory of seeing a musician. He was wearing his iPod.

The song that Calvin Myint was listening to was "Just Like Heaven," by the British rock band *The Cure*. It's a terrific song, actually. The meaning is a little opaque, and the Web is filled with earnest efforts to deconstruct it. Many are far-fetched, but some are right on point: It's about a tragic emotional disconnect. A man has found the woman of his dreams but can't express the depth of his feeling for her until she's gone. It's about failing to see the beauty of what's plainly in front of your eyes.

We are prone to that, aren't we? We get so caught up in busyness that we miss some of the best parts of life.

In my presentations, I often liken these little "best parts" to Cracker Jack® prizes. God has scattered these free prizes all around us: a watercolor sunset, the smell of fresh cut grass, the intricacy of a snowflake. We're so busy being self-absorbed and stressed-out that we miss them all because they're hidden just below the surface of our hurried consciousness. How sad must it be for the Creator of the Universe to have made all of these spectacular prizes for us to enjoy, while we mindlessly pass them by every single day. Brennan Manning writes along this same vein in *The Ragamuffin Gospel*:

> We get so preoccupied with ourselves, the words we speak, the plans and projects we conceive, that we become immune to the glory of creation. We barely notice the cloud passing over the moon or the dewdrops clinging to the rose petals. The ice on the pond comes and goes. The wild blackberries ripen and wither. The blackbird nests outside our bedroom window, but we don't see her. We avoid the cold and the heat. We refrigerate our-

selves in summer and entomb ourselves in plastic
in winter. We rake up every leaf as fast as it falls.

The reality of these words is heartbreakingly true.
But it wasn't always this way for us. We were all children
once. For *The Post* story points out:

> There was no ethnic or demographic pattern
> to distinguish the people who stayed to watch
> Bell, or the ones who gave money, from that vast
> majority who hurried on past, unheeding. Whites,
> blacks and Asians, young and old, men and wom-
> en, were represented in all three groups. But the
> behavior of one demographic remained absolutely
> consistent. Every single time a child walked past,
> he or she tried to stop and watch. And every single
> time, a parent scooted the kid away...

> ...The poet Billy Collins once laughingly observed
> that all babies are born with a knowledge of po-
> etry, because the lub-dub of the mother's heart
> is in iambic meter. Then, Collins said, life slowly
> starts to choke the poetry out of us. It may be
> true with music, too.

It saddens me to think of how many times I have ob-
sessively concerned myself with the trivial, while missing the magical. Oh, how tragically often do we trade the

Cracker Jack® prize for the peanuts?

The problem is a grave one. Edna Souza hails from Brazil and was shining shoes at L'Enfant Plaza the day Joshua Bell performed for an audience of ghosts. She knows the problem firsthand; she sees it every day.

> Souza was surprised to learn he was a famous musician, but not that people rushed blindly by him. That, she said, was predictable. "If something like this happened in Brazil, everyone would stand around to see. Not here."

> Souza nods sourly toward a spot near the top of the escalator: "Couple of years ago, a homeless guy died right there. He just lay down there and died. The police came, an ambulance came, and no one even stopped to see or slowed down to look.

> "People walk up the escalator, they look straight ahead. Mind your own business, eyes forward. Everyone is stressed. Do you know what I mean?"

The home page of Adultitis.org claims that Adultitis has transformed people into zombie-like doo doo heads. I marveled at my cleverness when I first wrote it, but now my stomach turns from its truth. The epidemic marches on, choking the beauty and value of life out of each successive generation. Its life-stealing grip is passed down to our children like some sort of twisted family tradition.

I believe there is hope. The choice for change is our own. Opportunities to turn the tide present themselves every day. Sometimes in the form of a violin virtuoso on your morning commute, sometimes in the form of free tickets from a stranger when you're tired and just want to go home. I am grateful that I took the opportunity to experience the concert Friday night, to drink in a moment I am richer for, and won't soon forget. The struggle against Adultitis is a daily one, but one worth fighting.

Gene Weingarten says in his *Post* article, "If we can't take the time out of our lives to stay a moment and listen to one of the best musicians on Earth play some of the best music ever written; if the surge of modern life so overpowers us that we are deaf and blind to something like that—then what else are we missing?"

An awful lot, it turns out.

Weingarten, Gene. "Pearls Before Breakfast." The Washington Post April 8, 2007: W10.

Manning, Brennan. The Ragamuffin Gospel Visual Edition: Good News for the Bedraggled, Beat-Up, and Burnt Out. Sisters, OR: Multnomah Books, 2005.

My Inner 5-year-old
by Kim

Last night we ended up at the Madison Symphony Orchestra. First time ever. Very cool.

During the experience, my mind was fluttering with thoughts and questions. I felt like I was five again, wondering all sorts of things.

Here are a few of the highlights…

1. This is a very long song. Longer than *November Rain* and *Stairway to Heaven* combined.
2. The cymbals guy is similar to the kicker in football. He has to wait and wait and wait and wait, and he'd better not mess up when his turn finally comes.
3. This hall looks like something out of *Star Wars*.

4. It's funny when they are all warming up at the same time. That really sounds terrible.
5. Did the guys playing the double bass start playing when they were little? Were the instruments bigger than they were?
6. How come everyone in the audience looks so serious? Are we not allowed to show that we're enjoying this?
7. How come the entire orchestra gave us a standing ovation at the end? All we did was sit here. They are the ones who deserve the standing "O."
8. I'd love to hear Statler & Waldorf's (the Muppet critics) thoughts on this.
9. I'd like to play the triangle.
10. We're sitting so close we may get sweated on by the musicians.
11. Who in the world could ever have the skills to write a symphony?
12. The guys have to wear tuxes but the ladies can get away with wearing anything black.
13. I love the oboe.
14. Try not to cough and/or sneeze during the "quiet parts." (I had a cold.)
15. What would happen if the conductor sneezed?
16. This is the most beautiful thing I've ever heard!

You Are in Perpetual Beta Mode

by Jason

Digital marketer Steve Rubel offered up the concept of life being a perpetual beta. For those of you non-techies out there, according to Wikipedia, "beta" is a concept used in the software industry to identify the first version of a program to be released outside the organization or community that develops the software, for the purposes of evaluation and testing.

Simply put, *if it's in beta mode, it ain't perfect.*

Life is in perpetual beta. What a great reminder to us all, especially those of us who struggle with the Adulti-tis-driven tendencies to 1) consider ourselves perfect, 2) strive to be perfect, or 3) at the very least, *appear* to be perfect.

Kids don't have any qualms about not being perfect. It doesn't seem to bother them much. They color outside the lines, spill things from time to time, and aren't all that concerned with wearing clothes that actually match. If they were serious about being perfect, I suppose they'd never learn how to walk or ride a bike (too much falling down).

Somewhere along the line, we get the idea that we have to have things figured out, and that everything has to go perfectly. We don't give ourselves permission to make mistakes, we throw tantrums when other people don't perform up to our standards, and we refrain from trying new things for fear that we might look foolish.

All this adds up to lots of stress and unhappiness.

We were taught growing up that nobody's perfect, and yet we live our lives as though we should be. Should we strive to do the best that we can? Of course. But don't kill yourself for perfection, because it ain't gonna happen. (Wow! Two instances of the non-word *ain't* in one article!—Make that THREE!)

I guarantee you'll stress less if you keep in mind that you're always in beta mode. Because as my friend Eliz Greene says, "It's not about perfection, it's about moving in the right direction."

"Software release life cycle." Wikipedia. June 14, 2007
    <http://en.wikipedia.org/wiki/Software_release_cycle#Beta>.

A Time and Place for Everything
by Kim

Today I had a very ironic experience. Jason and I hosted my parents this weekend. The weather was gorgeous, so we decided a lunch down at The Pier would be great. It's a restaurant connected to The Edgewater hotel in Madison. The tables are right on the edge of Lake Mendota, Madison's largest lake. It was one of those days when you just soak in everything: the sunshine, the breeze, the conversation, the jumping fish, the ducks, the kayakers and even the families nearby.

As we sat under the blue and white umbrella and decided what we wanted for lunch, my mom proudly shared that she was going to get rid of some Adultitis by eating dessert first! That is exactly what I did to accomplish one of *The Escape Plan* challenges. Ironically, challenge #11 is "You're Not The Boss of Me: Do something your parents would never let you do as a child." Even though my parents would never have allowed me to eat dessert first as a kid, my mom was now doing it right before my eyes. My head about blew up (in a good way)! It was so much fun to see her childlike smile and hear her giddy laugh as she ordered.

On this same pier, at the very same time, a young family (mom, dad, and two young boys) pulled their boat up and docked it for lunch. I happened to notice that Mom was in charge of the boys and Dad seemed rather distracted. Mom was in charge of the boys. Much of his visit to this beautiful spot was spent fiddling with his BlackBerry®. I'm pretty sure he didn't even notice the fish or the ducks or the kayakers.

At one point, his five-year-old son was trying to open the oversized umbrella attached to the table. It was quite a wrestling match, which the umbrella won, as the boy fell on the ground. All the while, the dad was typing away.

Later, the mom took the five-year-old inside, leaving the two-year-old (who was wearing a life jacket) with his dad. The child wandered away from the table, to a spot where his dad could not see him. He knelt down at the edge of the dock, trying to reach something below. Dad was on his phone. Immediately, a woman from a neighboring table who saw this happening got the dad's attention and he came over. His reaction was, "He would've floated."

There's a time and a place for everything.

Was it okay that my parents never allowed me to eat dessert first as a youngster? Yes! That's what makes it so much fun to do now, and made it even more fun to see my mom's experience.

Was it okay for that dad to be distracted by his technology on such a beautiful day spent with his even more beautiful family? No. That was sad to see. He was doing what so many of us do: take life (and people) for granted. In the blink of an eye, his kids will be grown-up and his work will still be there. A day like that day is priceless. I think about all of the fun Jason and I had with my parents. What a blessing to have these moments making memories with those we care about.

Make sure you take full advantage of them.

The time and the place is NOW.

Live Life On Purpose
by Jason

I heard a story about a man who died in a West Virginia coal mine accident, and it really got me thinking. As I recall, he was only two months away from retirement. What is interesting to me is that most often, such a story is treated as a tragedy, as in "Oh, he was so close…"

While it is a tragedy that he died in such a terrible way (not to mention the suffering the families went through), I think it's telling that the emphasis for most people is on how close he was to retirement, a date on the calendar.

They say life is all about the journey, not the destination. But we don't often live like that. Many of us gear our lives around some arbitrary date in the future, as if everything will be better when that point in time—that day on the calendar—comes. But what makes THAT day on the calendar any better or more important than THIS day on the calendar? Nothing. The only reality is that today is all we have, and that other day may never come.

I think that's why I'm proud of creating *The Escape Plan* with Kim. It's about embracing each day as it comes, with the joyful exuberance of a child. It's not about living for retirement, or for next year, or for that mystical day when everything will be better because (fill in the blank).

I want to live life on purpose.

No worries.

No regrets.

"Dream as if you'll live forever, and live as if you'll die tomorrow." —*James Dean*

Lost: Childhood
by Kim

Do kids these days really get to have a childhood? Having worked in a school, I have heard firsthand the debate between schools and parents about the amount of homework children receive. I'm all for working hard and succeeding in school, but, why do kids have to then go home and work more? Even most adults only work eight hours a day. This really bothers me.

Then there are the high-pressured high schools. Their students are not even nineteen years old, and they have full-blown Adultitis. Anand Vaishnav from *The Boston Globe* wrote an article entitled: 'Suburban High Schools Try to Ease Up on Teen Stress.' It is refreshing to see that some people are noticing that this is a problem.

"Society as a whole is creating a stressful environment," said Rena P. Mirkin, principal of Wellesley High. "It's not 'Are you achieving?' It's 'Are you achieving with five honors courses, eight clubs, two sports, and three community service activities?'"

Sadly, this is not just a problem for students in prep schools. I've seen this problem with five- and six-year-olds in my own kindergarten classroom. Karate on Mondays, dance on Tuesdays, swimming lessons on Wednesdays, Thursday they have a friend over for a "play date" (if they're lucky enough to be able to convince their parents to let them skip t-ball). This is insane. When do kids get to just hang out in the backyard and play?

How in the world can their imaginations and creativity develop if they are always in a structured environment? It's hard to imagine what's worse: parents signing up their small children for whatever the kids may think they NEED to be a part of (as if kids know what's best for themselves!), or parents who sit back passively watching their high schoolers join every team, club, and group, never leaving time to explore possible interests that might impact their career choices and ultimately their happiness in adulthood? (As if high schoolers know

> Adultitis is contagious, especially among family members.

what's best for themselves!)

Both sets of parents are blinded by their own Adulti-tis. They have such an extreme case themselves, they do not see how it is rubbing off on their children. This is wrong, and very sad. Be careful! Adultitis is contagious, especially among family members.

Don't let it bring your whole family down.

Vaishnav, Anand. "Suburban high schools try to ease up on teen stress." The Boston Globe July 31, 2005

Why the Rush?

by Jason

Our lives are busy. Busy, busy, busy! In fact, isn't it true that we use busyness as a badge of honor? As in:

"How's it going, Bob?"

"Great Stan. I've been really busy."

"That's good, Bob."

Meanwhile, Stan thinks to himself, "Bob is quite successful. He's a real go-getter. Every time I see him, he seems really busy."

It's as if whoever can prove they're the busiest wins (although I'm not sure what). It's rare that anyone bothers to ask what someone is busy doing. And it's rarer still that anyone would ever admit, "I haven't been very busy at all. I'm just taking life as it comes, enjoying it one moment at a time." In his insightful blog, marketing maven

Seth Godin offered this bit of honest persepctive:

> Last week, I was running from one meeting to another in the city when I passed an old friend on the street. "No time to talk, sorry!" I said as I hustled off.
>
> When we connected by email a bit later, he said he hoped I had a good meeting, and that it was worth the hustle.
>
> I couldn't remember where I had been headed.
>
> It seemed important at the time.

Sometimes we need to slow down and realize that the things we think are super urgent—the things that keep us oh so busy—really aren't.

Godin, Seth. "It seemed important at the time." Oct 4, 2006 <http://sethgodin.typepad.com/seths_blog/2006/10/it_seemed_impor.html>.

School of Fish
by Kim

Jason and I talk a lot about looking to children as teachers; miniature "sherpas" to show us how we should live a stress-free life guided by a childlike heart. We saw a sherpa the other day while walking into the Georgia Aquarium (the world's largest aquarium). She was about three years old and couldn't contain her excitement as she ran alongside her parents towards the entrance. She had bright pink tights, a colorful skirt, and black and pink cowboy boots. So cute! She was excited to be there. I can always learn a thing or two by observing the behavior of a sherpa.

As we commented on this bundle of enthusiasm ahead of us, neither of us realized that we would soon see sherpa-like behavior in those that live at the aquarium, the fish. They were the exact *opposite* of stressed. It was so peaceful watching the beluga whale swim upside down, without a care in the world. The playfulness of the sea otters made everyone smile. They were surrounded by toys, which the kids pointed out right away. I envied the calm and graceful movements of the sea turtle and the jellyfish. We even got to get rid of some of our own Adultitis in the touch pools, which housed stingrays, starfish, shrimp, horseshoe crabs, sharks, and sea anemones.

Who knew that the fish would teach me a few things about relaxing?

So, should we lie around and seemingly do "nothing" all day, like the fish? Not necessarily, but we should take the time on a regular basis to really relax and get to a place of mental, physical, and spiritual peace.

There's nothing fishy about that.

Are You On the Right Track?

by Jason

Being on the road can be tough. The adventure is fun, but lots of little "stuff" can add up and wear you down. Stuff like lugging heavy suitcases and extra boxes filled with books through the airport...waiting an hour on the runway for some last-minute plane repair to be documented...taking your shoes off for the hundredth time while a uniformed official looks at you suspiciously... being in so many different hotels that you forget which numbered door your room key will open...and trying desperately to catch a few moments of sleep on a red eye flight in a seat that seems more like a sardine can than a place to rest.

That's the "stuff" that can really take it out of you. Just yesterday, Kim and I were in four states in one day (North Carolina, Michigan, Wisconsin, and Minnesota).

But we actually like being on the road. The "stuff" is what we use to help us practice what we preach. It can be a challenge at times, but ultimately, it's the people we meet that make it all worthwhile.

In Chapel Hill, we met a young guy from Mexico named Carlos. He works with special needs kids and was in New Orleans when Hurricane Katrina hit. He was the *only* person in the whole audience who raised his hand when Kim asked if anyone had eaten dessert first in the last week. After our talk, he told us the reason he moved away from Mexico was because all of his friends were only concerned about looking and dressing a certain way. They mocked him because he was different. It's hard for me to imagine anyone not wanting to be friends with Carlos. He was different alright, but a refreshing kind of different. Were it not for his curly black beard, you'd swear you were talking to a little boy, full of life and fun.

We encountered a woman named Joyce at another gig. She seemed to hang on every word we said, with a wide smile beaming through the crowd. (Speakers love audience members like that.) When the presentation was over, she leapt to her feet for a standing ovation. She stopped briefly at the autograph table to enthusiastically thank us and kiss us both (for some reason I get lots of kisses from older women). We learned later, from someone who knew her well, that she had been in a bit of a depression. He told us that if nothing else, just to see her so uplifted made the whole event worthwhile.

We also had dinner with a talented musician named Bryan. We became friends over the Internet, and he drove two hours to see one of our presentations in Charlotte. At dinner we talked about big dreams. He shared how inspired he was by our *Escape Plan*, and that our message was a factor in his decision to give up a job in the computer industry that he didn't particularly like for his current role as youth minister and up-and-coming musician. It was a humbling experience and a fun time.

One of the neatest stories of all involved a woman who happened to win one of the free prizes we give out to lucky audience members. It involved finding a hidden toy capsule (similar to the free prizes we include in every Lemonade Stand order) that contained some sort of reminder—a souvenir—from childhood. After the presentation, she shared a remarkable story.

She and her family had just been in the Midwest to visit relatives and introduce her kids to the place where she grew up. She had really hoped to find a buckeye that she could show them. Her kids had never seen buckeyes, which were something she used to play with as a child. Naturally, the time went so fast that she didn't think of the buckeyes again until they were on the way home. She wanted to kick herself. As it turned out, in an audience of almost 200 people, she was the sole winner of a magazine and a toy capsule that just so happened to contain... a buckeye.

Those are just a few stories from our most recent road trip that remind me that we're on the right track. Those little "Godwinks," as SQuire Rushnell calls them, serve as signs to encourage and strengthen us amidst the less-than-fun "stuff" that can wear you down.

No matter what you do or where you work, everybody has "stuff" that is a little bit less than fun. But hopefully you have moments that remind you why you're doing what you're doing—those moments that give you joy and a sense of fulfillment.

Here's a hint: if experiences like these are few and far between, you might want to reconsider how you're spending your time.

Life As A Daring Adventure

by Jason

Kim and I are in Arizona this week. It's hotter than the inside of an Easy-Bake Oven.

After a speaking engagement in Scottsdale on Sunday, as I signed books for busy moms and teased little kids, I noticed an elderly woman standing quietly in the background. She looked like she was waiting for the crowd to clear out. Once the activity level died down, she and her walker made their way over to the table where I was sitting. "I want to share a story with you," she said eagerly.

Dorothy was her name, and she informed me matter-of-factly that she was eighty. Her wispy, silver hair framed her plump face and sparkling eyes.

"Ten years ago, I thought I was going to die," she started. "So I made a list of all the things I thought I was going to do 'some day.' One by one, I started doing them, you know, the things we always say we're going to do, like visiting someone, making a phone call, writing a letter."

One of the things Dorothy decided to do was book a flight to meet her brother for lunch. They didn't see each other very much; he never had the time and she never had the money. He took a half day off ("He never does that!") and picked her up at the airport. They had a delightful lunch with his wife and family.

"My brother is kind of a workaholic. For the life of him, he couldn't figure out why I was there," she said. "I told him, 'I'm here because I love you and I wanted to spend time with you.' It was probably the best gift I could have ever given him."

"And then I surprised my husband when I told him we were going to Hawaii," she continued. "'What?! You're crazy!' he said. 'People like us don't go to Hawaii.'"

A year later, they were in Hawaii.

I could see the childlike joy shine from her eyes as she described traveling to Italy for the opera, another life-long dream. "It was so wonderful!" she exclaimed. "They so love their opera over there. The old theater was beautiful, so opulent—and it was even an opera I knew!"

"I had so much fun doing all of those things," Dorothy continued. "I'm sure it was one of the reasons I was cured."

Now just minutes earlier, I had been encouraging a roomful of people to make the most of their days, slowing down enough to appreciate life's captivating details, and being brave enough to chase their dreams. But if everyone had had the chance to hear Dorothy tell her story and see firsthand the effervescent life in her blue eyes, my words wouldn't have been needed.

And I'd have been fine with it.

But instead, most people work late into the night, rushing around like pinballs in a noisy arcade game, desperately trying to keep up with an impossible standard, even though something deep inside yearns for something different. Sadly, it often takes a doctor telling you that your days are numbered before you begin to make some changes.

> Most people are rushing around like pinballs in a noisy arcade game.

And that's if you're lucky enough to get a warning.

I am more certain than ever that God intended our lives here on earth to be more like the one Dorothy described: exciting, invigorating, and filled with moments of wondrous awe and giddy delight.

I think that when we get to heaven, it might be like returning home from a long trip. The angels and the saints will crowd around us, eager to hear the tales of our life. "Who did you meet? Who captured your heart? What did you see? Wasn't the sunset over the ocean great? How impressive was that opera?" These are the questions they'll ask us, and they'll even be patient and sincere enough to want to see all our pictures and watch all of our home movies.

How sad would it be for them to hear you respond, "People like me don't do that sort of stuff."

Whatever is in your heart to do, do it. Write that letter. Make that call. Take that trip. Helen Keller was right when she said, "Life is either a daring adventure or nothing."

Live life daringly. You only get one.

You've-Got-Mail Cyber Challenge
by Kim

There is a cyber stress epidemic that is greatly contributing to Adultitis.

Checking email.

How many times do you check your email in one day? In one hour?

Be honest!

Are you excessive?

You just never know who might have some interesting or good news for you. You better check. It's like when you were little and always wanted to be the one to go get the mail from the mailbox. Maybe you'd actually receive mail on three out of 365 days, but it was still fun to check. That childlike optimism and curiosity can actually get you into trouble in the world of email. Email has a way of bringing stress of its own, including:

- Overflowing inboxes.
- Miscommunication due to brevity and misinterpretation of the written word.
- Wasting minutes (and hours) of your life deleting spam.
- Waiting for someone to reply who never received your email for some reason. (Somewhere in cyber space, I'm sure there are lost emails floating randomly about.)

Don't get me wrong, I'm not sure what my life would even look like without email, but most days I am convinced that it doesn't necessarily make my life easier.

A study about "email stress" revealed some fascinating and alarming numbers:

34% of the 200 workers questioned admitted to checking their inbox every 15 minutes. And though 64% of the workers said they looked at their emails more than once an hour, monitoring software showed that it was more like 40 times an hour. 34% of the workers also said that they were stressed by the sheer number of emails that come in, and the need for a speedy reply.

64% of workers check their email 40 times an hour!?

YIKES.

No wonder email is stressful.

Even if you are not one of the 64% who has a serious email addiction, it is safe to assume that you, like me, overcheck your mail, causing you to be distracted from many tasks throughout your day. We all have problems with our work being interrupted. It's time to stop this madness. Therefore, I am instituting the "You've-Got-Mail Cyber Challenge." For one week, you are only allowed to check and respond to email three times a day: morning, mid-day, and afternoon. No email in the evening. Instead, relax, read, have a conversation with a human, go on a walk, etc.

Can you do it?

If not, why not?

Are your excuses justified (life or death) or are they weak and derived from a secret addiction to the "Get Mail" button?

If you are struggling with a nasty case of Adultitis, this is a great first step. Give the challenge a try and let me know how it goes.

Ani, "Do you suffer from 'email stress'? ." Aug 14, 2007
    <http://www.rediff.com/getahead/2007/aug/14email.htm>.

So Long,
Crocodile Hunter
by Jason

When I first saw Steve Irwin, The Crocodile Hunter, I thought, "Now this guy is one big kid!" His boyish passion and wide-eyed enthusiasm were irresistible. Whether he was sticking his head in a crocodile's mouth or picking up an irritated snake by the tail, I couldn't stop watching.

He died doing what he loved, interacting with animals. For a few brief moments after learning of his passing, I couldn't help but think, "Why did he always have to put himself in danger all the time? After awhile, it was bound to catch up to him." But then I reconsidered. I would rather die at 44, passionately doing what I loved, than spend my whole life playing it safe so I could die at the age of 88 in a rocking chair.

As I speak nationwide about Adultitis, I often wonder if it's possible to live a life that's completely Adultitis-free. I must say, I observed this guy for a long time, and I couldn't find any definitive signs of the disease anywhere. I didn't know him personally, but even the people who knew him best say that the guy you saw on TV was the real Steve Irwin.

The man's curiosity, playfulness and passion were way off the chart. And he had a big dream. He wanted the world to see normally feared and despised animals like crocs, snakes and sharks as he saw them: cute, gorgeous, and beau-oooo-tiful. He reasoned that if people could relate to these creatures, they'd be more inclined to protect them and their habitats. Did he delight in the little things? Let me put it this way: I once saw him root through a pile of "komodo dragon poo" with the enthusiasm and excitement of a boy opening his only present on Christmas morning.

He's the perfect example of being childlike—I'll never forget his frisky grin or how his eyes got as wide as saucers when he stumbled upon a rattlesnake nest—without being childish. Besides being a committed dad and husband, he was more serious and determined than anyone to protect wildlife and educate us on the beauty and importance of all of God's creation.

We need more Steve Irwins in this world. And I'm not just talking about the wildlife community. We need someone who is as enthusiastic and energetic and optimistic and determined in the arena of politics. We need some Steve Irwins in the field of education. In dentistry. In the pharmaceutical lab. In the local bank. The most tragic thing about losing Steve Irwin is that there are too few people like him.

So long, Crocodile Hunter. Thank you for teaching us. Thank you for showing us what an Adultitis-free life looks like.

An Experience
So Grand

by Jason

I'm not sure it's possible to explain the Grand Canyon experience in words. Or pictures. Or anything else, for that matter. Talk about an escape from adulthood and all its worries and stresses!

The ride north from Phoenix was a treat in and of itself. We took the "scenic" route through Prescott, Jerome, and Sedona. In the desert, the cacti looked like prickly green fingers pointing to the bright blue sky. As our elevation increased, the rock formations reminded me of old men with wrinkled faces and sunburned cheeks, looking over the pine trees, which were standing at full attention like a million green soldiers. And Sedona's horizon reminded me of an inferno, set ablaze by its famous fiery red rocks.

But all of that was just an appetizer for the feast that was to come. I have never had such little use for a camera in my life. Oh sure, I took a zillion photos, but after each shot, a glance at the viewfinder left me terribly disappointed.

It was fascinating to see everyone else furiously trying to record the experience, too. It made me smile at our humanness. Overwhelmed at the sight before us, we struggled to preserve with our cameras what words could not. But it was all in vain; capturing the beauty, the breadth, the brilliance of the Grand Canyon with a camera is like trying to recite the alphabet with only two letters. If a picture is worth a thousand words, then it's about nine hundred, ninety-nine thousand short.

> Capturing the beauty, the breadth, the brilliance of the Grand Canyon with a camera is like trying to recite the alphabet with only two letters.

We were lucky to experience many highlights during our short stay. One was the chance to see the sunset and the sunrise over a natural wonder that is known for its sculpted rock formations. Trust me, though, the light is the real superstar. As the sun was setting, a gentle rain fell in the canyon, affording us one of the most brilliant rainbows I have ever seen.

Another highlight was the opportunity to see a motion picture about the Grand Canyon—the most watched IMAX movie of all time. During it, I was amused as the narrator pondered the canyon's mysterious origins. "Did it come from the hand of God, or was it a work of nature?" he asked. Questions like that always make me laugh. As if it's an either/or proposition. Who do they think created nature?

A night earlier, after I had finished giving the keynote presentation at the Catholic Cemetery Convention (one of my most interesting gigs, to be sure), Kim and I had occasion to do some stargazing. The Marriott offered the complimentary experience, hosted by a real-life astronomer with a pretty nice telescope. We got to see the moon up close and personal, and Jupiter and a few of its moons, too.

These encounters with the stars and the canyon made me feel smaller than I ever have before, yet so sure of the existence of God. Sometimes I wonder why He bothers at all with the human race; but then again, His ways are not my ways. His magnificent creation testifies to that.

Experiences like sitting on the edge of the Grand Canyon and gazing into the starry depths of the universe really take me back to childhood, that time when everything was new, and big, and awesome. Curiosity was limitless; you could never know enough.

As we get older, we often take on this cocky, unimpressionable, I've-seen-everything attitude. Nature—God's nature—has the ability to knock us off our pedestal, reminding us that we are not as big as we think we are, but also to assure us that there is an order to everything. And that even in the desert, there is life, and there is hope.

Stress Begets Stress
by Kim

Remember Jeff Foxworthy's, "You might be a red-neck if..." routine? Classic! In our speaking gigs we often help audiences identify their Adultitis by giving some examples in a similar way. For instance, you might have Adultitis if...you consider your cell phone to be a body part. You might have Adultitis if...it's dark when you leave home in the morning and it's dark when you get home, and you don't live in Alaska.

This last one is quite an issue. I happened upon an article talking about the trend of commuters leaving earlier and earlier, while also leaving work later in the day to avoid the traffic, only to find themselves pulling twelve- to thirteen-hour days.

Adultitis, much?

> In 2000, 1 worker in 9 was out the door by 6
> a.m., the new data says; by 2006, it was 1 in 8.
> That might not seem like a big change, but it has
> put more than 2.7 million additional drivers—for a
> total of 15 million—on pre-dawn patrol.

On paper, it makes sense to beat the rush and feel less stressed. In reality, however, lifestyles are becoming more pressured because of the adjustments that need to be made in order to accommodate to this shift: earlier bedtimes (taking away from evening recreation and relaxation), later dinners (leading to a more stressful and shortened family time), and a decrease in exercise due to the lack of opportunity. All of this is done in an effort to avoid the tension of the commute. What a mess. It's a vicious cycle of stress.

One woman featured in the article said that she has to leave home at 6 a.m. and doesn't leave work until 6 p.m. to avoid the traffic. She has a two-year-old daughter and she and her husband are unsure about having more children because of the challenge in taking care of one. They depend on her parents and in-laws to watch the little one. They've learned to build the long days into their lifestyle. "We just try and make it work," she says. "My husband is very supportive of my career. He's offered to move close to my workplace, but I just really enjoy where we live."

It sounds like she hardly has time to actually live there. Looks like a classic case of living for the weekends.

Another example in the article was much more refreshing. A guy from New Jersey leaves at 5:15 a.m. each morning to get into Manhattan for work, but instead of going right to work he goes running in Central Park, then to the gym to work out and shower, all before arriving at work at nine. He is a marathon runner and uses this early morning time to train.

If your life is a stressed-out mess, it's time to stop blaming your circumstances.

He shares, "I could've chosen the path of 'woe is me' and fight the traffic and let it destroy my life. Instead, I've turned it around and made it a positive for my health and a hobby I enjoy greatly."

How refreshing!

You can create positive things from the challenges in your day-to-day life. Last year, Jason and I met a great couple from Los Angeles who have made it their mission to provide "Practical Audio Training for People on the Go." By creating *Freeway Guides*, they are encouraging commuters to use that time for self-improvement. In addition to using these guides, you could also learn a second language, or even catch up on your favorite podcast.

The lesson here is simple. YOU are in charge of your life. If it's a stressed-out mess, it's time to stop blaming your circumstances and start moving towards change.

What does your daily schedule look like?

Are you finding a good balance between work, family and alone time?

What can you do to take more control of your life, for the good of your health and sanity, as well as your relationships?

Copeland, Larry, Haya El Nasser and Paul Overberg. "As commutes begin earlier, new daily routines emerge." USA Today Sep 12, 2007.

New Eyes
by Jason

"The real voyage of discovery consists not in seeking new landscapes but in having new eyes."
–Marcel Proust

By default, children are born into this world with new eyes. That's why they get so excited by the little things. Years of living can build up thin layers of film over our perspective. Our vision gets cloudy; life becomes a boring shade of gray.

Part of what it means to escape adulthood is not to seek ever more elaborate and expensive experiences, but to wake up to the small treasures all around you and see the world with new eyes.

I'll Have What They're Having
by Jason

Last night I had a chance to partake in a little fireworks action. Kim and I have an ongoing debate: she'd prefer that they shoot 'em all off in the span of about 10 seconds. I, on the other hand, like when they're spread out a little bit so I can savor them, you know, like a fine wine. (But not too much; my hometown liked spreading them out so much you could read a few pages of the dictionary between each explosion.)

[Digression alert] By the way, have you ever noticed that fireworks on TV are unbelievably terrible? On the surface, it seems like a good match: television easily delivers the sights and the sounds—the two primary elements, right? Well, this morning I saw a newscast this morning close with the very same grand finale I saw last evening. I thought to myself, "That's nothing like what I experienced last night." Then it hit me: they're missing the feel of the fireworks. It's just not the real deal unless you can feel the big booms rattle your bones. And that's why I think fireworks on TV suck. [End of digression.]

Anyhoo, one of the highlights of last night was a row of small kids—kindergarten age—sitting behind us on the curb. Through most of the show, they screamed and cheered as the fireworks exploded across the sky like electric party favors. At one point, Kim asked me, "Can you imagine being so excited by this that your natural inclination is to cheer at the top of your lungs?"

> Can you imagine being so excited that your natural inclination was to cheer at the top of your lungs?

No. No, I can't. But it seemed like fun.

Somewhere along the line, most of us lose that unbridled childlike enthusiasm. Now I'm not sure even I'd want to live in a world where everyone, everywhere cheered anytime something remotely exciting happened. (Although it might be fun: My Cherry Coke came with TWO cherries! Yeehaaaa!!!)

A jump to such an extreme might be a bit much for the mainstream. But it would be nice if someone (Jones

Soda, maybe?) could extract that highly-concentrated childlike cheer and create a diluted version for the masses. Maybe eventually we could up the dosage, but I'm betting just a tiny spoonful would make a big difference. (I know a few people who might be killed by just a drop of the stuff.)

I don't know much about bottling soft drinks, but I can offer this reminder: life can be a lot of fun. Let's try and shed this "been there, done that, got the t-shirt" attitude we get as we get older. Let's make a point to celebrate the little things.

Maybe even with a woo hoo or a yippee skippee every once in a while.

Eeyore or Tigger?
by Kim

As I sat typing on Daisy, my Mac, waiting for the car to get some fresh oil, I couldn't help but smile at the psychology lesson that was unfolding right before my eyes. Folks were coming in to drop off their cars for everything from oil changes to big money repairs. To say that "attitude is everything" at the car mechanic's is an understatement.

First, a thirty-something woman came in, acting very Eeyore-like. Although she wasn't elderly, she seemed to be moving at a pace that would get her some significant discounts at Old Country Buffet. Her presence was gloomy and grey, just like America's favorite depressed donkey. The cheery voice behind the counter asked her how her day was starting. She responded with a weary, "Not horrible, I guess. I'm just tired." God bless him, the determined optimist joked, "Well, at least you're not sick AND tired."

No laugh.

Shortly thereafter, a baby-boomer gentleman came bouncing through the door with a smile on his face and a friendly salutation that extended to everyone in the room. It was such a stark contrast, I stopped working to take notice. This guy was larger than life. He brought the sunshine in with him. It was clear in my quick assessment that he loved living, was confident and purpose-driven, and that he was going to have a great day, no matter what. He seemed be living Tigger's philosophy: "Bouncing is what Tiggers do best."

Do you have a storm cloud lingering overhead or a rainbow?

Which one are you?

Look above you right now. Do you have a storm cloud lingering overhead or a rainbow?

Look on your desk, is your glass half full or half empty (or bone dry)?

The harsh reality is that within three seconds of encountering someone new, you are evaluated. First impressions are made and they're almost impossible to reverse. Sure, life isn't all daisies and roses, but how quickly do you bounce back?

Rainbows and storm clouds exist in the same sky. One secret to keeping that rainbow above you is to surround yourself with positive people. As motivational guru Jim Rohn says, "You are the average of the five people you spend the most time with."

My friend, Rich "the big kid" DiGirolamo, ends all of his emails with, "Make something fun happen today! The world needs it!" And then there's my buddy, Phil Gerbyshak, the "Make It Great!" guy. He's constantly encouraging others to "Make every day a Great Day!"

Look around you. Are your "five people" bouncing or trudging through life?

If someone saw you at the mechanic's, what first impression would you make?

Take charge of your attitude.

It might be time for a tune-up.

Silly Ideas
by Jason

As I travel around the country encouraging people to escape adulthood, I am always mindful of the people who look at me suspiciously. These are the ones who think that "escaping adulthood" is the perogative of the irresponsible few; those undergoing a midlife crisis with a few screws loose to boot.

I read an article from *The Boston Globe,* about a 45-year-old writer named Peter Lewis who built a tree-house in his backyard. A glorious, wonderful, 250-square-foot, two-story structure featuring a wood-burning stove and a retractable staircase "to keep the girls out." Lewis, uses the house as a getaway—a place to get some work done. And sneak in a few naps.

However, the article pointed out:

> Lewis is adamant that he didn't build the treehouse as the result of a midlife crisis. He didn't do it to learn how to be a kid again, he says, because he has never stopped being one. And though it was a great and sometimes overwhelmingly difficult experience, he wouldn't describe it as cathartic. "I tried to come up with some deep, philosophical reason for building the treehouse, but it was just a silly idea and I felt like doing it. Fortunately, I had a very understanding wife and enough scrap to pull it off."

Lewis was also fortunate to have the example of his parents. In the article, he acknowledges:

> "My parents were both very creative people who thought way outside the box. Mom told me that dreaming was important and that dreaming big was what set people apart." The catch, she told him, is to act on those dreams. "In other words," he says, "go ahead and think up great and sometimes odd ideas, but then make them happen."

For more on Peter's treehouse, you might want to check out the coffee table book, *Treehouse Chronicles: One Man's Dream of Life Aloft.*

All of us have at least one silly, childlike idea in the back of our mind that goes unpursued because we're afraid. We're scared that people might think we're nuts.

Here's a newsflash: *we're all nuts.*

But shelving a dream because you're afraid of what other people might think is **REALLY** nuts. That's our problem. That's why everybody is so stressed-out: everybody is going nuts because they're afraid to do what they *really* want for fear that people will think they're nuts. Got it?

Here's to dreaming big and following through on "silly" ideas.

Go nuts.

Donelan, Jenny. "Aerie tale." <u>The Boston Globe</u> Oct, 20, 2005.

The Contradiction of Being Childlike

by Jason

The other day, a woman came up to me after one of my presentations in Pleasanton, California.

"The whole time you were asking rhetorical questions, I found myself trying to figure out the answers," she started. "For instance, 'What is the point in our lives when we lose our childlike spirit?' Sometimes I think it's when we're forced to shoulder the load of life's responsibilities; we're afraid that we won't be able to handle them adequately—or that we'll be seen as irresponsible—if we hold on to our childlike side."

You know, I think she's right. Too often, accepting the responsibilities of life is approached as an all or nothing proposition. Either you effectively manage your life by embracing a decidedly measured and strict "grown-up" approach, or spiral into a socially unacceptable life of immaturity, aimless wandering, unfulfilled potential and unpaid bills.

But I don't think it's an all-or-nothing choice. I believe it's possible to be childlike, have fun, and enjoy life while still being a responsible and successful mom, dad, boss, teacher, employee, or even President of the United States.

Take, for example, Jennifer Robinson. She's a cool friend of mine who also happens to be smart as a whip. (Are whips smart? Where did that phrase come from?) Anyhoo, she has a Ph.D. in Industrial Engineering and is co-founder and Chief Operating Officer of FabTime Inc., a company specializing in cycle time management software for wafer fabs.

I have no idea what that means.

From a simpleton's perspective, that seems like a very grown-up job with little room for childlike hijinks. (Notice I said "seems like"...I happen to know that engineers can be quite a goofy bunch in their own right.)

So even though Jennifer's day job seems potentially strait-laced, she writes an incredibly thorough blog dedicated to promoting the love of books by children, and the continued reading of children's books by adults.

That's right, children's books.

Life is filled with contradictions, and it's a fruitless —but seemingly innate—activity that we humans like to engage in: labeling things and putting them in boxes. Contrary to popular belief, there are gay people who work for the Catholic Church, liberals who are pro-life, and Republicans who care about poor people. Life is not always all or nothing. It is possible to be childlike AND still pay your bills with real money, not the Monopoly® kind.

That's the lifestyle that I advocate. One that actually gives you a better chance of reaching your full personal potential, and also guarantees that you'll have fun along the way.

Paper or Plastic?
by Kim

I officially hate grocery shopping.

I went this morning and I found myself advancing rapidly from a calmly curable Stage 1 Adultitis (due to early-morning grumpiness) to a severe, full-blown case of the disease. I think I would rather be sitting in a dentist chair.

So, instead of dreading it every time our stomachs are growling, I am choosing to change my strategy a bit. How can I avoid the dark grumpy rain clouds that form over my head each time I am grabbing that cart? I looked online for some ideas only to be very disappointed. Either I am the only one who hates grocery shopping or I am the only one looking to do something about it.

Realizing that I was on my own to find some helpful hints for supermarketphobes, I consulted my inner child. Without further ado, here are my 8 ways to survive grocery shopping:

1. Dodge the crowds. If at all possible, shop on a weekday either early in the morning or late in the evening. If you have to shop at peak times, try to hit the places that give free samples. For some reason, getting that little piece of toaster oven baked frozen pizza helps take the sting out of the experience.

2. Reward yourself. Buy a "treat." How many times as a child did you beg your parents for that impulse buy at the checkout? Cut out the middleman and appreciate one of the perks of being an adult. Get that Snickers® bar for the ride home.

3. If possible, do online grocery shopping. There are lots of services out there now that will deliver your goodies to your front door. Most of the programs online even save your grocery lists from one month to the next.

4. Bring some tunes. I'm always envious of those teeny-boppers who are toting their iPods everywhere. Because they are going through puberty, society al-

lows them to be anti-social by listening to music in public, but really, who is being offended if I wear earbuds in aisle 5? So, why not hum along with your favorite Christmas songs while you pick out your produce?

5. Avoid budget remorse. "They" say if you make a list and stick to it, you will have the best chance of staying within your means. It's bad enough that you have to carry the heavy grocery bags at the end. You don't need the extra weight of feeling bad about the amount you spent.

6. Schedule a date. Invite a friend to join you and make it an event. Maybe even pick up some over-priced coffee drinks on the way. Chat, laugh, and shop.

7. Adios, kiddos! Let's not fool ourselves, children and grocery stores were never meant to mix. Swap kids with a friend during your shopping times or schedule your trips when your spouse or babysitter can help out. If you must take the youngsters, keep them busy.

8. Find a fun hat, shirt, or pair of shoes to wear only when you are shopping. You will find yourself look-

ing forward to wearing that, no matter where you will be. I wore my snazzy winter hat with the tassels on top this morning. I always get a few smiles.

When Life is Like a Jar of Muddy Water
by Jason

Kim and I are kicking around the idea of taking a week off to do absolutely NOTHING. To be honest, I'd love to be locked in a lakeside cabin up north somewhere, but at this moment, we don't have the funds to do anything fancy like that. If it happens, it'll probably be a low-tech, in-house sort of thing. No phones, no TV, maybe even no email. Right now, the idea is as frightening as it is tempting—a whole week off? The company will surely implode, won't it?

The reality is that, in order to work smarter, we need a little time to detox. Somehow our society has gotten the idea that "busy" is good and admirable, a sign that we're successful. As I mention in *Escape Adulthood*, even our vacations are hectic: Gotta do and see everything you possibly can, right? Busy vacations can be fun, but our bodies (and souls) need some quiet time, too.

It's like we're jars of muddy water. When we're busy and in constant motion, things can get pretty cloudy. But if we take the time to sit for a bit, the dirt settles, and life gets clearer. You can shake the jar as forcefully as you want (work harder), but until you actually STOP, you won't be able to see clearly, allowing yourself to work smarter.

In an article on thestar.com, Ruth Liew makes some really good points. She accurately points out that adults have an aversion to silence:

> Many people are stressed out in their daily lives. They are unable to gain composure. Anxiety rises when they try to be tranquil. They get worried when there is silence. They need to be in a room that is filled with sounds from all directions. They chatter away without thinking much about what they are saying.
>
> Most adults get anxious when it gets too quiet. Joggers wear headphones and listen to music as they exercise in the mornings. Some restaurants have television sets mounted in every corner. We

carry our mobile phones wherever we go.

Young children like a quiet hideaway place. Sometimes this place is in a discarded box or a space under the stairs or a wardrobe. Some children crawl under the bed or the dining table and imagine they are in another, faraway place.

When children are given free time, they tend to achieve more because they are not stressed by demands. I remember watching a precocious three-year-old who seemed a little "lost" in her nursery school. While the other children were in their respective classrooms, she would lie down on a large cushion and perform her own soliloquies.

She would say, "I don't know why I don't have any friends. I like them but they don't like me. What shall I do?" After uttering those words, she got up and went to meet her peers in the next room. She had worked it all out by herself. Children discover their inner selves when they retreat from the hustle and bustle of daily life.

While the article focused on children, and how important it is for parents to allow their kids opportunities for quiet, I think the lesson is applicable to all of us.

When life gets muddy and out of control, the secret to clarity is to find a secret hideaway place, slow down, and shut up.

Liew, Ruth. "Quest for quietness." Mar 23, 2006 <http://thestar.com.my/ lifestyle/story.asp?file=/2006/3/23/lifeparenting/13733251&sec= lifeparenting>.

Keep Asking Why
by Jason

How is it that kids have so little life experience, yet often blow us away when it comes to wisdom? I found a great list of tips from children written by Eolake Stobble-house. Here are my top 10 favorites:

Making your bed is a waste of time.

If you want to draw on the wall, do it behind the sofa.

Don't drink anything when you're upside down.

Don't tell your mother her diet isn't working.

Don't ask your three-year-old brother to hold a tomato.

If you want a cat, start by asking for a horse.

Don't sneeze when somebody is cutting your hair.

When Mom is upset with Dad, don't let her comb your hair.

Don't let a dog stand guard over your food.

And my all-time favorite:

Keep asking "why" until you understand it.

The Gooey Gray Gift
by Kim

This morning as I was leaving church, I remembered that the priest had mentioned that there would be cement trucks outside, getting ready to pour new sidewalks. On the way to my car, I passed a "seasoned" citizen parking himself about a foot from the area that would soon contain freshly poured concrete. He purposefully put his hands on his hips and looked on with great anticipation, as if it were 9:15 p.m. on the 4th of July.

I got to my car and started to drive away. Then I heard the cement truck start up, so I glanced back. Much to my surprise, I found that the concrete show now had quite the audience. No less than ten inquisitive seniors were in attendance. The curious crowd was social proof that something cool was about to happen...and all the while my car continued to drive past them.

What has happened to my childlike curiosity? On my drive home, I thought about how cool it would've been to see that gooey gray cement plop into the frames on the ground.

Living with curiosity is a gift, a gift that many of us leave dusty and faded in childhood. Try to rediscover this gift today. As modeled by those eager seniors who had managed to retain their childlike curiosity, it brings joy and excitement beyond words.

NASA Has Adultitis
by Jason

In 1962, in a speech given at Rice University in Texas, President John F. Kennedy challenged our nation to put a man on the moon:

> We choose to go to the moon. We choose to go to the moon in this decade and do the other things, not because they are easy, but because they are hard, because that goal will serve to organize and measure the best of our energies and skills, because that challenge is one that we are willing to accept, one we are unwilling to postpone, and one which we intend to win.

If I were to say, my fellow citizens, that we shall send to the moon, 240,000 miles away from the control station in Houston, a giant rocket more than 300 feet tall, the length of this football field, made of new metal alloys, some of which have not yet been invented, capable of standing heat and stresses several times more than have ever been experienced, fitted together with a precision better than the finest watch, carrying all the equipment needed for propulsion, guidance, control, communications, food and survival, on an untried mission, to an unknown celestial body, and then return it safely to earth, re-entering the atmosphere at speeds of over 25,000 miles per hour, causing heat about half that of the temperature of the sun–almost as hot as it is here today–and do all this, and do it right, and do it first before this decade is out–then we must be bold.

However, I think we're going to do it, and I think that we must pay what needs to be paid. I don't think we ought to waste any money, but I think we ought to do the job. And this will be done in the decade of the sixties. It may be done while some of you are still here at school at this college and university. It will be done during the term of office of some of the people who sit here on this platform. But it will be done. And it will be done before the end of this decade.

JFK's "Moon Speech" was unprecedented. It was outrageous. Its childlike audacity captured the imagination and wonder of millions of Americans. And in 1969, we made it true.

Sadly, today, NASA is inflicted with a serious case of Adultitis. It has abandoned the entrepreneurial spirit of space travel. That spirit is now with the people who were kids when Neil Armstrong first walked on the moon—the people who are investing their own money developing private spacecrafts. According to Charles Lurio, a space consultant, "The current American space program is a passive activity that has no connection with those watching it or their children."

In an article on reveries.com, NASA's Sean O'Keefe sees it just a bit differently: "If I had authorized somebody to jump into a plastic airplane fueled by laughing gas in just a flight suit, there would have been a Congressional investigation the next day—whether it was successful or not."

As kids, we all start out with big dreams and great passions. Eventually, Adultitis can get its stranglehold on us and we lose that magical spirit. In the sixties, NASA was a kid. Now it's a crotchety old grown-up, mired in politics and boring "adultlike" thinking. Cheers to the ones who have carried on NASA's once-great childlike spirit by pushing forward in the quest to develop personal spacecrafts. Maybe these entrepreneurs have more money than sense. Maybe they're driven by ego. Maybe they're crazy.

But at least they don't have Adultitis.

Manners, Tim. "reveries - cool news of the day." June 17, 2005
    <http://reveries.com/cool_news/2005/june/jun_17a.html>.

Pajama Run
by Kim

Imagine with me for a few minutes...

You're seven years old and lying in bed after a full day of playing four square, drilling on spelling words, and practicing your cursive. Life is good. After getting your goodnight kiss from mom, you imagine what the next day will bring. Then, out of nowhere, like a bolt of lightning, your door flies open with the sound of pots and pans being beaten like the Notre Dame fight song. You pop up, knocking over the water by your bedside. "Pajama Run!" your parents exclaim, as they stand in your room telling you and your sister to get up and get moving!

Woo hoo, a Pajama Run!

You put on your slippers and coat, but are not allowed to change into regular clothes—that's the whole point. No wonder mom asked you to wear your new pajamas tonight, you laugh to yourself! Dad will not divulge the final destination, even though you beg him to tell you.

You hop into the station wagon and zoom off to a local ice cream joint, where you are invited to order a sweet treat—in your pajamas! Sitting in the Twisty Station, you and your family laugh as you recall the looks on your faces, how your sister had no idea what was going on, and how funny it was that you spilled your water. You also recall that you *did* notice Mom setting the pans on the counter before bed, but thought maybe she was just getting ready for the morning. Lots of giggles all around! As you eat your sweet treat you announce to your family that when you get big and have a family, you are for sure going to take your kids on Pajama Runs!

This is what I imagined when a woman at one of our gigs described her family's tradition. She shared that this is a fun way that they escape adulthood. She also mentioned that sometimes everyone in her children's small school will go on a Pajama Run together. They all meet at a predetermined place and time. The kids are thrilled to see their friends there, also in pajamas.

There's nothing better than to sit in your pj's out in public, enjoying a banana split, way past your bedtime! It keeps things interesting, playful and spontaneous.

Make a Pajama Run tonight!

Second Childhood
by Kim

The other day, a woman left a heartwarming comment that made me smile, regarding my post about the Pajama Run. She basically summarized the message of Kim & Jason in a few insightful words. TadMack shared,

> Sometimes stuff like this makes me tearful, and I think, 'Dang! I want a do-over! I didn't get a childhood like that!'...and then a little light goes on. OH. See you at the ice cream parlor. I'll be the one with the curlers and the cloud-printed flannels...

Some people have amazingly magical childhoods to reflect upon, and others simply do not. Unfortunately, for many grown-ups, the reality of their childhood is such that it should never be relived. Our message is for everyone, not just those with the warm, fuzzy memories. As Jason shares in one of his books, the good news is that we were all born with certain "secrets" from childhood. They are instinctual and often just need to be dusted off and put into practice, even if you never got the chance the first time around. A quote I read the other day says it well: "It's never too late to have a happy childhood. But the second one is up to you and no one else."

So, if the second one is up to you, what are you doing about it?

Are you carefree?

Are you playing on a regular basis?

Are you appreciating the little delights around you?

Are you authentic?

Are you dreaming big dreams?

Are you laughing often?

Are you constantly learning and growing?

Are you honest?

Are you believing that people are good and things work out for the best?

Are you living with passion and perspective?

The choice is yours and no one else's.

Enjoy your do-over!

The Best Day Ever
by Jason

Imagine standing in front of a room filled with one thousand people. You ask if they consider themselves optimistic. How many people raise their hands?

Yep, all of them.

Everybody thinks of themselves as optimistic; nobody will admit that they are pessimistic. When pressed by someone who knows them and thinks otherwise, they might admit, "I'm not pessimistic. I'm realistic." You'll never hear anyone say, "Yeah, that's me, pessimistic. I see the worst in every situation, my best days are way behind me, yesterday will always be better than tomorrow, and if anything can go wrong, it most certainly will."

So, if we extended our imaginary survey to, say, the whole world, we'd have a planet packed with self-proclaimed optimists, right?

Riiiiiiigghht.

It's impossible to ascertain whether someone is an optimist or a pessimist just by asking her. But that doesn't mean there isn't a way to distinguish between the two. And it's foolproof, too.

Listen to the words they use.

The language a person uses will reveal whether or not they really are the optimist they believe to be. If you start listening attentively, you'll understand what I mean in no time. Take, for instance, the simple act of asking someone how he's doing. Will he respond with a cheerful, "Great! Never been better!" or the more common, "Not bad. Could be better," "I'm hanging in there," "I could do without the heat," or "If it wasn't for all this snow, I'd be fine."

Judging a person to be optimistic or pessimistic by listening to them speak is like playing poker against someone with his cards facing out. Easy.

I've read *The Power of Positive Thinking* by Norman Vincent Peale many times. The classic book covers several timeless truths, among them being the notion that when we use more positive words, we will think more positive thoughts, and more positive outcomes will be the result. If you boil it all down, Dr. Peale really wrote a book about Adultitis. He was trying to get people to be more childlike! After all, how many pessimistic five-year-olds have you been around? Kids believe that TODAY has the potential to be the best day ever, that the prize in their Cracker Jack® could be worth a million dollars, and that Santa will be able to squeeze that new bike—and his jolly plump frame—down the chimney with nary a problem.

As we get older, Adultitis creeps in and poisons our language, which breeds negative thoughts (and negative results). But there is hope. That optimistic five-year-old is still within you. You need to bring him or her out by changing the way you talk. Practice weeding out negative words and peppering your language with words of abundance, prosperity, and optimism—even if you don't believe them. Maybe instead of thinking of that little gadget that wakes you up every morning as an alarm clock, why not start thinking of it as an "opportunity clock," as Zig Ziglar suggests. Keep at this game of putting a positive slant on the words you use, and eventually you WILL notice some differences. Just like Dorothy leaving black-and-white Kansas and entering the Technicolor world of Oz, that inner-five-year old will awaken and you'll see the world in a whole new way. You'll realize that today really IS the best day ever.

And people won't need to wonder if you're optimistic or pessimistic. They'll already know.

Making Time for Play
by Kim

I have a confession to make. I am addicted to getting my picture taken with fun characters, such as Bucky, the mascot of the University of Wisconsin, or a statue of Ronald McDonald.

I know this could err on the childish side of the spectrum, but I argue that it's my playful childlike side that motivates the addiction.

Here's the scenario: Jason and I are out and about and we see a "friend," as I like to call them. "Quick, Jason! Get the camera!" I exclaim. Within seconds, I have captured a memory that will make its way to iPhoto, destined to stay there forever.

This is an example of being playful.

I was thrilled to find out that the first class I would

take for my major in college would be "The Importance of Play." "Early Childhood Education is the major for me," I thought. Much of the homework for the class involved playing, and doing things I liked to do…like playing frisbee and swinging at the park. The professor was awesome! I'm sure you're assuming it was the best blow-off class ever, but I really learned a lot that semester; and it opened my eyes to the importance of play for everyone, not just for 3- to 5-year-olds.

Adults assume that play has to either be done with children or else it comes in the form of a structured activity or sport: playing golf, tennis, or video games. The essence of play, however, lies in making the choice to do something you enjoy.

> The essence of play lies in making the choice to do something you enjoy.

You get to decide what's important to you, to use your own creative thoughts and energy.

Play is something that brings you joy and enables your mind to relax and move away from worries and stress. Examples could be cooking, knitting, woodworking, gardening, reading, scrapbooking, playing the piano, and even getting your picture taken with some "friends."

Do you carve out at least 30-60 minutes a day for play? Playing a game that your kids or grandkids choose does NOT count. It has to be something that YOU select.

If you decide to play Monopoly and they join you, then that's fine.

Please tell me that, like me, you have a confession to make regarding play. If you don't, then here's one for you: "I don't make time to play, but I know I need to."

Admitting you have a problem is the first step to recovery.

Ignite that childlike joy with some play today. You won't regret it.

Pro Choice
by Jason

I once wrote about the phenomenon of people settling for unrewarding careers and jobs. I listed a bunch of reasons—I call them excuses—that people give for this interesting but overwhelmingly common condition. I proposed the idea that no one has to settle for an unrewarding, passionless work life.

Not surprisingly, I was accused of being unrealistic and—gasp—idealistic!

I have always loathed being called idealistic. Depending on the source, I considered it an insult, because normally, when someone calls you "idealistic," it's his way of saying, "You have no clue. Your ideas are irrelevant, if not completely ridiculous."

However, being labeled idealistic puts me in pretty good company. What in the world is wrong with being idealistic? Jesus was probably the most idealistic person who ever lived. Martin Luther King, Jr. ranks up there pretty high, too. Same with Gandhi, Mother Teresa, Walt Disney, Bono, and pretty much anyone else who's ever made a positive difference in the world. Starting today, I've decided to take being called idealistic as a compliment.

What I find most interesting is how desperately people try to convince me (and more importantly themselves) that when it comes to having a rewarding career, they are different. Try as they might and wish all they want, they don't have any choice but to remain where they are.

Now, don't get me wrong. You may wish you could do something else, but upon considering the sacrifices and steps required to make it happen, decide to stay put. I'm fine with that; it's your choice. But don't try to tell me you don't have options.

I heard a speaker the other day say something like this: "All successful people are 'causationalists.' They are the CAUSE of the positive results in their life. Unsuccessful people blame their lack of success as an EFFECT of the things other people do to them or don't do for them."

Successful people know that things happen in life

that are out of our control. But they also know that when it comes to success, those outside influences add up to less than 10% of the big picture. The vast majority of our roadblocks come from within. Responsibility for your happiness and success lies squarely on your shoulders. If you're not happily living a passionate, successful life, you're the one to blame. I guess that's why it's easier to pretend you don't have any alternatives.

The reality is that you do have choices, although they may not be easy, ideal, comfortable, safe, quick, cheap, simple, popular or fun.

Pretending you don't have them is just wrong.

Marshmallows and Motorcycle Trips
by Jason

A few years ago, I had the privilege of addressing a group of elementary and high school teachers at a district wide meeting in Stark County, Illinois. I like talking to teachers. Rarely do they have people standing up for them, acknowledging all the hard work they do, and reminding them of why they got into teaching in the first place.

It was the first day back from Christmas break, and frankly, I don't think anyone was too excited to be there. (At least that's what Kim's teaching experience has taught me.) After I promised that I wouldn't say a word about curriculum, and had everyone complete a short questionnaire that I call an Adultitis intake, I am confident to say that we had a pretty good time.

A high school science teacher, Al Curry, was the winner of the Chubby Bunny contest. He stuffed at least five jumbo marshmallows into his mouth and was still able to perfectly enunciate the phrase, "chubby bunny."

The group enjoyed Al's confident display of marshmallow domination, and I had a great conversation with him after the presentation. He told me about one of the ways he manages to remain Adultitis-free. Every summer, he and his college-age son go on a motorcycle trip. Their biggest expense is gas, as the duo eats cheap and sleeps in tents. They've seen a lot of the beautiful wide-open spaces of this country, including Yellowstone, the Badlands, and scenic Minnesota. The Grand Canyon is at the top of their wish list.

Al related a story about a trip his son took to a leadership camp in Washington, D.C. when he was in high school. According to Al's son, there were a lot of well-off Ivy League kids there. A discussion came up about what kinds of cars everybody had, and names like BMW and Mercedes surfaced. The kids were aghast to learn that Al's son didn't own a car.

"I have an old motorcycle, though," he sheepishly offered.

"You do?"

"Yep. Me and my dad go riding every summer."

That led to an hour-long discussion about the summer road trips. The East Coast kids were mesmerized. According to Al—and I think he's right—his son's new friends were probably not as interested in the stories of the road as much as they were perplexed by the concept of actually having quality time with Dad.

They say time is money. I don't know about that. All too often in today's world, parents try to substitute money—and BMWs—for time, as if they were an equal swap. It never ceases to amaze me that no matter how young or close to adulthood a child is, he or she would always rather have time than money.

Today is as good a time as any to look at your supply of time and money, and re-evaluate how you're investing each of them. How do you spend your time? How do you spend your money? You can always make more money, yet no one has figured out how to make more time. When it's gone, it's gone.

No one has figured out how to make more time.

Brand new BMW: $35,000.

Ivy League Education: $150,000.

A motorcycle trip to the Grand Canyon with your son: Priceless.

Cramming for Kindergarten
by Kim

Have you ever read something that immediately made you feel sick to your stomach? This is how I felt when I finished the article, 'Cramming For Kindergarten,' featured on CBSnews.com. I think the title gives you an idea of what road I am going down. Yet another example of adults, and in this case, parents, passing on their Adultitis to their little ones. Tragic! The article talks about parents who have chosen to seek out tutors for their pre-schoolers, in order to help them "be ready" for the academic demands of kindergarten. One of the parents shared:

"It wasn't that she (her four-year-old daughter) had any kind of limitations. It was that she really wasn't interested, and she needed to be motivated a little more. It is unfortunate that you have to do all this preparation for kindergarten, but you really do."

Really? Do you?...Why? How many "motivated" four-year-olds have you seen lately? Not every child wants to read at age four or even shows interest in letters, numbers or writing this early. Sure, the child may have a little catching up to do with her ABC's when school starts, but will she need a tutor to help her run on the playground or use her imagination in the house area or dig a tunnel at the sand table or laugh with a friend?

One may argue that this parent cannot be faulted for wanting what is best for her child. I would argue that the best thing for a preschooler to do, in order to "be ready" for school, is to BE A KID.

The homework looks like this: catch bugs, sneak some cookie dough from the bowl, jump in the biggest puddle you can find with your "good" clothes on, play hide-and-seek and scream when someone finds you, let a dog lick your face until you can't stop laughing, hide out in a tent made of blankets and couch cushions, master the art of the Kool-Aid® and milk mustaches, make Play-Doh® snakes, grow a bubble beard in the bath, lose your way in a wild story, get goosebumps when your parents kiss you goodnight, fly a kite, get muddy, enjoy the scratchy sound of your training wheels, fingerpaint, play "house," and my personal favorite: swing!

Heck, I'm trying my hardest to get back to this life now. The creativity, the innovation, the imagination, the perspective—so pure and innocent. It is a true tragedy to see this stolen from the little ones who teach us so much about life.

Morales, Tatiana. "Cramming For Kindergarten." CBS News. Aug 12, 2005
    <http://www.cbsnews.com/stories/2005/08/11/earlyshow/living/
    studyhall/main772750.shtml>.

8 Ways to Prevent a Cardiac Event

by Jason

The Duke University Medical Center published a report in the Jan. 15, 2002 issue of the American Journal of Cardiology, confirming that stress management appears to reduce the long-term chances of heart patients having another "cardiac event," and also provides an immediate and significant cost savings.

The team found a financial benefit of stress management strategies within the first year of the study. Average costs for patients who utilized stress management were $1,228 per patient during the first year, as compared to $2,352 per patient for those who exercised and $4,523 per patient for those who received usual care.

The medical center defines a cardiac event as "bypass surgery, angioplasty, heart attack or death."

Kind of a weird term, if you ask me. My grandfather died of a heart attack when he was pretty young. I can just imagine the people at his funeral saying, "That was one heck of a cardiac event."

The results of this heady scientific research project seem pretty obvious to me, but I guess that wasn't the case for the National Institutes of Health, who issued three grants for the study. I'm also not sure that we need to provide massive stress management programs to teach people something that once was second nature to us. I don't see too many children dropping dead from "cardiac events," do you?

At the risk of sounding overly simplistic, here are 8 simple and free ways to help prevent "cardiac events":

1. Laugh. The average preschooler laughs 450 times per day. The average adult laughs just 15 times per day. Quit taking yourself so seriously.

2. Take a Walk. Exercise is important, but it's not a choice between daily sweatfests at the gym or nothing. Take the stairs instead of the elevator. Park farther away at the supermarket. Lose the riding lawnmower. (Unless you're in charge of keeping the local football field in tip-top shape.)

3. Take a Bubble Bath. When was the last time you did that?

4. Get 8 Hours of Sleep. Or at least seven.

5. Take Frequent Naps. You may or may not want to pull a George Costanza and sleep under your desk (if you do, pack an alarm clock), but you can rekindle the trend of taking Saturday afternoon naps. Check the TV for golf—you'll be out like a light.

6. Use Babysitters. You deserve a night to yourself.

7. Be Off When You're Off. When you're at work, work hard. But when you're off work, let it go. Don't think about it. Learn to shut down that part of your mind for a day or two, and you'll be amazed at how productive you become.

8. Laugh. I know, I know, I mentioned this one already. But that preschooler is kicking your butt—you've got 434 more laughs to go.

A New Ism
by Kim

Racism, ageism, sexism—these are all wrong and should never be tolerated. On our plane ride home from Tampa the other day, I witnessed a new "ism," which I've labeled "kidism." I define kidism as prejudice or discrimination against people who are acting like kids. With ageism, the discrimination is directly related to the age of the person; with kidism the prejudice is based on the target's behavior. Victims of kidism can be both children and adults.

The man who was exercising kidism was sitting next to me. He sat reading his paper for a while. After about twenty minutes, the child in front of him, who was about four years old, started to play. I'm not sure what the boy was doing; but he was talking and giggling at an appropriate volume level. He seemed to be having fun, which quickly shows up on the radar screen of those who are kidist. After about a minute, the man leaned forward, tapped the back of the boy's seat, and asked him to "keep it down up there, please." The part of this situation that points to kidism is that the child was not being excessively loud. If the child had been an adult having a conversation with his neighbor, he would not have been any louder. So, why did the man have to tell him to "keep it down?"

This is an example of kidism.

There is a fine line between adults who are exhibiting kidism and those who are annoyed by out-of-control children. Believe me, I've been the latter. When parents take their offspring out in public, it is like putting their parenting skills on display for all to see. Children "test" their parents in public; they try to get away with things and push boundaries. Parents who cannot control their children in public are in a whole different category than what I am referring to.

Adults with severe cases of Adultitis, like the man on the plane, have a hard time being around someone who is acting like a kid because of their extreme distance from this playful nature. They most likely don't even know they are living with Adultitis, so they are unaware of why they are reacting in this way. They typically cannot stand the company of others who are enjoying the little things, being playful, and living with passion. They have allowed Adultitis to take over and cloud their perspective on happiness. These are the unfortunate folks living with "full-blown" cases of Adultitis.

I guess the best way to fight this prejudice is to be a living example of one who can "be a kid," whether we are four or forty-four. Who says we have to acquire and maintain stuffy fuddy-duddiness once we are officially members of adulthood?

Being an adult isn't the problem. It's letting go of "being a kid" that gets us into trouble.

A Happy Birthday
by Jason

My family assembled at my brother's apartment in Madison for my dad's 52nd birthday party. We all chipped in for a brand new DVD player. His old one was out of commission because "someone" inadvertently put in two DVDs at once. DVD players don't like that. When the disgruntled machine refused to eject the discs, Dad decided to take matters into his own hands and disassemble the thing. And, as life will teach you, taking something apart is much easier than putting it back together. Thus the need for the new DVD player.

But I digress.

I was exceptionally surprised by a gesture my parents made shortly after dinner. They said that they had been thinking about my book, which brought to mind the birthday parties of childhood. When a kid has a birthday party and invites his or her friends, they reasoned, usually the guests get some type of party favor. So they decided that in an effort to "return to childhood," they would provide favors for all of their guests.

From a rather large cardboard box, my father pulled out little Darth Vader bags jammed with colorful treasures: gummy candy in the shapes of cafeteria food, a Star Wars® Pez® dispenser, Razzles®, and long candy necklaces for the girls and foam disc guns for the boys. Everyone got one: my brothers and their wives, my two nieces, Kim and me.

I'll tell you what: that was one of the funnest (I know, not a word) birthday parties I've been to in a long time. The gesture might have seemed cheesy to an outsider; but we had great fun digging into the bags, surveying the loot, trading Pez dispensers, and biting into gummy pizzas. It was a little thing, but it really added a lot to the evening. I highly recommend goody bags for your next party, particularly if there aren't any kids around. People may give you strange looks at first, but it won't be long before the five-year-olds inside them start puffing excitedly on those cheap—but fun!—paper blowout thingys.

Way to go, Mom and Dad.

Real Sophistication
by Kim

When one becomes an adult, it's assumed that your higher level of knowledge and reasoning brings a certain level of sophistication. Jim Henson saw this differently:

> "The most sophisticated people I know—inside they're all children. We never really lose a certain sense we had when we were kids." *–Jim Henson*

I think I know what he's talking about. I recently witnessed three grown men exemplifying Mr. Henson's version of sophistication.

Today I spied a man, about mid-40's, in a suit and tie, sneaking some notes on a hotel lobby piano. His face was aglow with a childlike smile.

The other day I spotted a man driving a convertible at 6:15 a.m. wearing a Santa hat.

A few weeks ago, I drove past a Harley enthusiast decked out in leather from head-to-toe, with a stuffed bear strapped to the back of his motorcycle.

By whose standards do you measure true sophistication?

A Lesson From Curious George

by Jason

I saw the movie *Curious George* recently. I really liked it. The animation was simple, with its own unique style; different from the hi-tech, hyper-realistic animation that is so common these days. The super great soundtrack by Jack Johnson added a pleasant and whimsical unity to the whole thing. The story, of course, was about the little monkey created by Margret and H.A. Rey. It was fairly formulaic, as many movies of this kind are, but still a fun way to spend an hour and a half.

I soon became aware that an underlying theme appeared quite often throughout the picture: Adultitis. Many of the characters had it in varying degrees. Almost all except George himself.

In *Escape Adulthood*, I talk at length about the importance of curiosity. It is my observation that curiosity burns long and hot in children, before it's slowly snuffed out as years go by. Many of us stop asking questions, questions like "Why?" and "Why not?"

I suppose one of the reasons for this is because we don't want word to get out that we don't know everything. Better to act like you've got it all figured out than to risk looking like a fool. Another reason might be that, even though change is constant, we like to resist it as much as we can. Change is not comfortable; so we avoid asking questions that lead to answers that might require it. Too often we engage in this pride-protecting, comfort-keeping behavior without really considering the consequences.

Marketing guru Seth Godin has an interesting commentary on how we get so wrapped up in the status quo, and go so long without asking questions, that we lose sight of the reason we started doing something a certain way to begin with. He wrote in his blog:

> The reason that you have a water bubbler in your office is that it used to be difficult to filter water effectively.

> The reason the typewriter keyboard is in a weird order is that original typewriters jammed, and

they needed to rearrange the letters to keep common letters far apart.

The reason we don't have school in the summer is so our kids can help with farmwork. Or because it's too hot and there's no air conditioning...

The reason you go to a building to go to work every day is that steam or water power used to turn a giant winch-like structure that went right through the factory building. Every workman used that power to do his work. As factories got more sophisticated, it remained efficient to move the workers, not the stuff.

People who take the time to be curious, to ask the questions no one else is asking, can open up doors of wonderful opportunity for themselves—or their businesses—and save or gain time and money. So take a cue from George and get curious. Why do you do what you do?

The reasons may surprise you.

Godin, Seth. "The Reason." Feb 15, 2006 <http://sethgodin.typepad.com/seths_blog/2006/02/the_reason.html>.

Soundtrack of Life
by Kim

The other day I had the privilege of seeing three individuals using music to escape adulthood.

First, there was a young blonde woman driving along the highway in her cute VW Beetle, with flowers popping up over the dash. Even though I couldn't hear her, she was obviously enjoying singing her tunes as she made her morning commute.

I saw the next person at the local grocery store. It appeared that he was working for one of the bread companies, and he was there early in the morning stocking the shelves with fresh loaves. He was sporting his iPod and grooving to the music, as he carefully placed each loaf on the shelf. He had a little smile on his face as he mouthed the words.

Later, a middle-aged guy wearing a striped tie pulled up beside me as I waited for the red light to turn. He was drumming on the steering wheel. He wasn't "just drumming," he was rockin'. It was fun to see.

Seeing these three people in the same day helped me to recognize how the simple act of listening to music can help manage Adultitis. If you add a little tuneage to some bland, routine tasks, they'll get done with a bit more fun.

Coldplay can help you clean the toilet.

Harry Connick, Jr. can assist you as you make your house payment.

Lionel Richie will be happy to help take care of that dirty laundry.

Madonna can help get you through the crazy morning traffic.

Little did you know, your favorite musicians are there to keep your Adultitis at bay.

A Lesson in the Little Things
by Jason

Tonight Kim and I had the privilege of babysitting our goddaughter Isabella. We took a field trip to the park. Upon arriving, I did the typical grown-up thing: scope the playground equipment in search of the most fun, unique, "big budget" installation. We grown-ups are naturally geared to skip past the things that appear ho hum. It's that "been there, done that" thing we're so good at.

Of course I expected that Belle would follow suit and make a beeline for the big multi-slide, suspension-bridged, plastic edifice.

Nope. Belle went straight for the pebble gravel. Crouching down, she stroked her hands through the tiny rocks, feeling the texture with her outstretched fingers. Then she grabbed a handful, stood up, and let the cool stones rain through her fingers. That occupied her for several minutes. Eventually, she did make her way to all of the playground equipment—including the gigantic structure o' fun—but the seemingly mundane objects seemed to captivate her the most.

Sometimes it takes a child to remind us to snap out of our preconceived perceptions and notice the often-overlooked details in life. The little things we are so quick to skip by can be the most interesting things of all.

Make a Joyful Noise
by Kim

Today began as an ordinary Sunday morning at church.

The opening hymn was starting as the priest and altar servers were walking up the aisle. As they approached the altar, I noticed that they had a visitor.

A young girl, not even 4 years old, had followed them up there. She was dancing freely to the music with a big grin on her face. She danced and danced for what seemed like minutes, but was probably only ten seconds. Then she did something that surprised us even more! She went up to the podium and grabbed the microphone, yanked it down to her level and sang her own version of the opening song. In a matter of seconds, the priest whisked her away from the microphone; and her embarrassed mom hurried to the front and helped her off the altar.

We were all a little shocked; and most of us were left smiling from ear-to-ear and wondering, "What just happened?" It certainly wasn't the normal routine for the opening song. This child had spirit! (Understatement of the century!)

It was an obvious example of childlike joy and spontaneity, which left me wondering where my spirit has gone. No, it's not socially appropriate to run up in front of everyone and sing and dance during a church service. However, I find myself struggling with spontaneity. It's a very childlike quality.

Something tells me that this little girl did not plan her adventure ahead of time. She just felt like dancing and singing "on stage," and so she did.

I think this went beyond youthful spirit; it was the purest picture of childlike joy.

And what a joyful noise it was.

How to Have a Mental Breakdown

by Jason

Never before has such a thorough, step-by-step guide to your very own mental breakdown been published, be it online or off. If you can master these easy-to-follow instructions, you too can be the envy of all your friends and find yourself well on your way to a life you've only dreamed of!

1. Treat traffic jams exactly as they are: carefully planned and sinister conspiracies designed to keep you from reaching your destination.

2. Pack your day so full that you are not distracted by

superficial things like the sunset, the smell of roses, or the toddler smiling at you from across the grocery aisle.

3. Avoid the time-wasting activity known as sleep. For best results, try to keep it under four or five hours per night.

4. Take everything seriously, because, obviously, it is.

5. Don't fall into the trap of expecting big, amazing, wonderful things to happen. They probably won't and you'll just end up disappointed anyway. And while you're at it, pat yourself on the back for out-growing the silly practice of believing in things like Santa Claus, the Tooth Fairy, and God.

6. Make sure you eat most meals either in the car, near the microwave, or from your recliner. If someone invites you to join them for a dinner that is likely to last more than fifteen minutes, respectfully decline.

7. Don't bother asking questions. You probably know all the answers anyway. If you don't, just act like you do. And remember, "Because we've always done it this way" is a perfectly good answer to almost every question.

8. You can take some time for yourself, but only if you're caught up on all of your work, your email inbox is completely empty, your bills are paid, and your junk mail has all been alphabetically sorted. And the grass has been cut.

9. If someone drags you on some sort of "vacation," be sure to take your beeper. Also, figure out the total time you'll be on said "vacation" and plan enough activities to accommodate double or triple that time.

10. Spend most of your waking hours—remember, you should be shooting for about 20 of those per day—doing things that completely drain you. You know, the stuff you'd never do in a million years if they didn't pay you such a good salary.

11. If all else fails, and you forget the other guidelines, a handy shortcut is to observe a child and do the exact opposite.

12. And finally, refrain from reading this book.

Finding the Golden Ticket
by Kim

The other day, Jason and I were talking with some friends about the wisdom that is gained by a near-death experience, a life-threatening illness, or the death of a loved one. Jason posed the question, "Is it possible to trick yourself into having that experience without really having it?" Wouldn't it be great to learn the lessons that those events give us without having to go through them?

Then I ran across some wonderfully wise words from a dying 40-year-old Florida man. I'd like to share them to pass along the inspiration I gained from his wisdom. This is a great example of the clarity of thought that one gains when faced with their mortality.

Today we have higher buildings and wider high-ways, but shorter temperaments and narrower points of view.

We spend more, but enjoy less. We have bigger houses, but smaller families. We have more com-promises, but less time. We have more knowledge, but less judgment. We have more medicines, but less health.

We have multiplied our possessions, but reduced our values.

We talk much, we love only a little, and we hate too much.

We reach the moon and come back, but we find it troublesome to cross our own street and meet our neighbors.

We have conquered the outer space, but not our inner space.

We have higher income, but less morals. These are times with more liberty, but less joy. With much more food, but less nutrition.

These are days in which two salaries come home, but divorces increase. These are times of finer houses, but more broken homes.

That's why I propose that as of today:

You do not keep anything for a special occasion, because every day that you live is a special occasion.

Search for knowledge, read more, sit on your front porch and admire the view without paying attention to the weeds.

Pass more time with your family.

Eat your favorite food.

Visit the place you love.

Life is a chain of moments of enjoyment, it isn't only survival.

Use your crystal goblets.

Do not save your best perfume, and use it every time you feel you want it.

Take out from your vocabulary phrases like "one of these days" and "someday."

Let's write that letter we thought of writing "one of these days."

Let's tell our families and friends how much we love them.

Never pass up a chance at adding laughter and joy to your life; every day, hour, and minutes are special. And you never know if it will be your last...

These words make me feel like I've found the "golden ticket." It helps me put things in perspective and gives me permission to make sure I am enjoying each moment. I think we all have these nuggets of wisdom (kind of like the chocolate nuggets in a Wonka® candy bar) within us somewhere, and it often takes a tragedy for us to fully recognize them. Can we really conquer our inner space without being faced with our final days?

I'm sure going to try...maybe if I eat a lot of chocolate that will help.

The Sin of Staying in the Wrong Job

by Jason

Look around you. There's a host of people working in jobs that are, shall we say, less than rewarding. If it were not true, the acronym T.G.I.F. wouldn't exist. Of course, the reasons most people give are legion: "I have a family to support"…"We need the benefits"…"This is all I know"…"It's a tough job market, I'm better off staying where I am"…"I've only got a few more years to retirement"…"We couldn't afford a pay cut"…"I'm too young"…"I'm too old"…"I don't know the right people"…and on and on.

I argue that, although perfectly admirable, these reasons are really an excuse to stay in one's comfort zone.

They are usually offered up as if another job—one that taps more deeply into our interests and passions—could never support a family, provide benefits, or mean a salary increase. And, more times than not, when someone offers up one of these excuses—I mean reasons—everyone else politely smiles and nods in a way that says, "Yes, this is a very wise and responsible person."

Wise? Responsible? *Really?*

I believe the key to a truly happy and fulfilled life is spending a good chunk of time pursuing the things you're passionate about. The things that really fire you up. The things you're good at. The kinds of things you'd do whether you got paid or not. The lie is that it's not really work if you're having fun. The truth is that there are more ways to earn a living doing what you're passionate about than you've ever considered.

> The lie is that it's not really work if you're having fun.

Now, given my stance on this subject, even I was blown away when I came across a quote from a fellow by the name of Arthur Miller. He said, "It is wrong, *it is sin*, to accept or remain in a position that you know is a mismatch for you. Perhaps it's a form of sin you've never even considered—the sin of staying in the wrong job. But God did not place you on this Earth to waste away your years in labor that does not employ his design or purpose for your life, no matter how much you may be getting paid for it."

Miller's point comes from a religious point of view, but I think it's still a relevant question for anyone to ponder: Are you wasting away your years? As I said at the outset, there's a host of people working in less-than-rewarding jobs.

Are you one of them?

The Secret to a Good Night's Sleep

by Jason

Is any time of the day a good time to watch the news? I don't know about you, but whenever I do so, I end up feeling angry, or sad, or frustrated, or disappointed, or overwhelmed, or hopeless, or some combination of the above. Most news telecasts are very early in the morning, or very late at night.

Do I really want to start my day with an order of doom and a side of gloom?

Or, for that matter, why would I want to finish off my day with big dollop of cynicism on top?

In one of our podcasts, Kim and I spoke with Jen Robinson on the topic of children's books. Jen mentioned that she almost always ended her day with a little bit of reading. Kim noted the irony of how children often wind up their days with a parent reading them a story, while many adults go to sleep after watching the evening news. Maybe that's why, according to the National Sleep Foundation, approximately 70 million people in the United States are affected by a sleep problem. The Adultitis monster is no longer under our beds...it has taken up residence in our heads.

Jen said that one of the things she likes about children's books is that the characters and stories seem so epic and heroic. It's hard to get that from 10-second soundbytes on the evening wrapup.

What would the world look like, as Kim asked during the interview, if everyone finished their day with stories filled with big dreams, happy endings, and good triumphing over evil? Would our sleep problems go down? Would the morning commute be more cheerful, or at least more civil? Would families be stronger, students more eager, and CEOs more likely to do the right thing?

I wonder.

> What would the world look like if everyone finished their day with stories filled with big dreams, happy endings, and good triumphing over evil?

I'm not advocating that we bury our heads in the sand, ignoring the reality around us. But is the news really reality, anyway? I see more jerks, idiots, and malcontents on one evening's broadcast than I do in a whole month of actually living my life. Besides, I have a pretty good idea of what's going on, even though I rarely catch the telecasts. The important things have a way of getting our attention.

It would be cool to see the effects of an entire nation trading in the evening news for a few pages of a good children's book.

Looking For Some Fun
by Kim

What's your favorite flavor of ice cream? See if you are in good company...

THE 10 MOST POPULAR ICE CREAM FLAVORS

1. Vanilla, 29%
2. Chocolate, 8.9%
3. Butter pecan, 5.3%
4. Strawberry, 5.3%
5. Neapolitan, 4.2%
6. Chocolate chip, 3.9%
7. French vanilla, 3.8%
8. Cookies and cream, 3.6%
9. Vanilla fudge ripple, 2.6%
10. Praline pecan, 1.7%

Source: International Ice Cream Associaton

We had an annual math lesson in my kindergarten class where we would make a graph recording the students' favorite ice cream flavors. It never failed; the same flavor won by a landslide five years in a row.

Blue Moon.

As you might expect, it's bright blue. Blue Moon came out on top because it is fun, not because it tastes the best to five-year-olds. I can't help but notice that it's not on the list of top ten flavors.

When I was little we would occasionally make our way into Baskin-Robbins® for a treat. With 31 flavors, there were lots to choose from. I don't believe Blue Moon was a choice, but Pink Bubblegum was (and still is). It is a dazzling pink with candy coated pieces of bubblegum (like Chiclets®). This chocoholic from birth would always order pink bubblegum. Why? It was fun!

Kids are perpetually seeking fun. What about you? Are you still looking for fun? Even if you say you are, does your day-to-day life serve as proof? If so, I bet people (kids especially) are naturally drawn to you.

Fun doesn't just happen…you have to work at it. What are you going to do to bring some fun into your life today?

Are you enjoying a vanilla cone or Blue Moon?

Are You a Fool?
by Jason

Well, you should be. We hesitate to ask questions because we don't want to look foolish. And then we wonder why success seems to come so easily to other people around us. Asking questions is risky. It can make us appear foolish to those around us. And most frighteningly of all, the answers to the questions might upset the whole dang apple cart. Scary stuff. But asking questions is the only way to grow your business, grow your faith, or grow yourself.

> "Go around asking a lot of damn fool questions and taking chances. Only through curiosity can we discover opportunities, and only by gambling can we take advantage of them." –*Clarence Birdseye, inventor and father of the frozen food industry*

Crazy Horse
by Kim

Today on my walk, I saw something that sparked a warm memory. It was one of those toy rocking horses suspended on springs.

Did you ever ride one as a kid?

My horse was faded and the springs were very loose from the many rides my three older sisters took over the years prior to my arrival.

When I would go for a gallop, Id experience a very specific combination of feelings. It was a little bit scary, a little risky because I wasn't in control. It felt like at any given moment I could fall off, because it was pretty shaky. The reckless, topsy-turvy feeling made me nervous, but I always enjoyed it. I wanted the adventure.

Kids have a way of identifying the danger in an activity and trying it anyway. Everything is new to them, so overcoming fear is a natural part of their everyday lives.

How is it that, when we grow past four feet tall, fear also seems to grow; and the pros of the adventure don't seem worth the risks involved?

As grown-ups struggling with Adultitis, we "need" comfort.

Everyone talks about the comfort zone, about stepping out, but I don't see very many people actually doing it. I don't think it's a "zone" that you step beyond. I think it's a wild and crazy horse ride. You have to jump on, embrace the adventure, accept the fear, and keep riding.

We all think that we need to stay in control. Well, the fact is that we are not in control. We will never be. The sooner we figure that out, the better we can give our lives to a bigger cause, to surrender to who we were meant to be...not to who we think we *should* be or who society *tells* us we should be.

We all need an adventure. We were made for more than this. I know I was. I know we all are.

Seeing that horse inspires me to embrace that childlike courage that I've left behind. I want to jump on my crazy horse—yes, the one that is rusty and unwieldy.

Giddy up, horsie!

Living Naturally
by Jason

Ever see a four-year-old walk into a room and declare, "Man! I am soooooo stressed out!"?

Me neither.

There are a multitude of reasons that little kids aren't stressed-out and inches away from little heart attacks, but one of them is because they tend to listen to their bodies. Mind you, this doesn't happen consciously. Rather, they have the tendency to go with the flow, letting their bodies dictate when to go and when to crash. Fiction author Robin Brande calls this "living naturally." In a blog post, she paints a wonderful picture of a friend's daughter as an atom: pure energy. At one moment, the little girl is dancing with her dog and plowing through the living room on her tricycle; the next moment she crashes in her father's lap and is out like a light. Robin observes:

> That's the most natural living any of us gets to see, the kind of living done by little kids and puppies. They eat when they're hungry, they eat everything they need, they run around and use up all their energy to the very last drop, and then they sleep...They just live the way their bodies and minds and spirits tell them to live, moment to moment.

How true that is. Kids don't need coffee to get themselves going in the morning or to keep themselves awake so they can finish one more project. Americans are famous for putting in long work days, but I can't help but wonder why, given all the time spent working, our quality isn't always on par with the best in the world. Maybe we're not listening to our bodies and we're trying to do too much. Maybe we need to get back to basics and follow Robin's example:

> Yesterday after our hike I came home, took a shower, and crawled into bed. And slept for three solid hours. I didn't worry about whether it would ruin my sleep that night, or what was going to happen with all that laundry out there waiting for me or that thick Sunday newspaper that needed

reading. I turned off the phone, got in my jammies, took the mother of all naps.

What a happy girl was I.

Then spent the next few hours sitting in bed reading a book. Just like I didn't care anymore! Just like I was a little girl again.

Just like I was allowed to.

Because I am. Because we all are.

That's one of the best things about being a grown-up. We're actually allowed to do these sorts of things. The problem is we don't act like it. We have this little devil on our shoulder—carrying a full-blown case of Adultitis, by the way—telling us that we'll ruin our sleep for the night, we'll blow our diet and gain seven hundred pounds, the laundry won't wash itself, our boss will fire us for not being more responsible, we'll miss an important phone call from Ed McMahon, blah, blah, blah.

I'm in the permission business. If you'd like to, as Robin suggests, "Return to your roots as a 3 1/2-year-old and have chocolate milk and naptime and a few fish sticks if that's what takes your fancy", I hereby give you official permission.

You're a grown-up now. You have the power. Now go start acting more like a kid.

Brande, Robin. "To live that naturally." June 18, 2007
    <http://robinbrande.com/life/to-live-that-naturally>.

Hands-Free Addiction
by Kim

Warning sign that you might be taking yourself too seriously: there's a cell phone in your ear, but you aren't talking to anyone.

And you aren't even expecting a call.

Don't get me wrong. I love the idea of hands-free cell phones. They are safe for driving and make typing much more convenient. Using them makes sense in a lot of situations, but when I see someone with a cell phone in her ear in a restaurant with her husband, I can't help but wonder. I just hope she's an emergency responder or waiting for a call from her best friend who is about to go into labor.

One thing I know for sure: if we take ourselves too se-

184 Kim & Jason Kotecki

riously, life will be sure to humble us—publicly. Whether it's Charmin® on your shoe or a mysterious black thingy in your teeth that you discover with horror while looking in the mirror hours after dinner, rest assured, it will happen.

So please, take the cell phone out of your ear and truly "be" in the moment.

Collect More Grass Stains

by Jason

Here are a few poignant tidbits from the article *If I Had My Life to Live Over*, written by American humorist Erma Bombeck:

I would have burned the pink candle sculpted like a rose before it melted in storage.

I would have invited friends over to dinner even if the carpet was stained, or the sofa faded.

I would have eaten the popcorn in the 'good' living room and worried much less about the dirt when someone wanted to light a fire in the fireplace.

I would never have insisted the car windows be rolled up on a summer day because my hair had just been teased and sprayed.

I would have sat on the lawn with my new clothes and not worried about grass stains. I would have cried and laughed less while watching television and more while watching life.

I would never have bought anything just because it was practical, wouldn't show soil, or was guaranteed to last a lifetime.

Instead of wishing away nine months of pregnancy, I'd have cherished every moment and realized that the wonderment growing inside me was the only chance in life to assist God in a miracle. When my kids kissed me impetuously, I would never have said, Later. Now go get washed up for dinner. There would have been more I love you's. More I'm sorry's.

But mostly, given another shot at life, I would seize every minute...look at it and really see it, live it, and never give it back.

Don't worry about who doesn't like you, who has more, or who's doing what.

Instead, cherish the relationships you have with those who love you.

These words were written by a woman dying of cancer. And they really sum up beautifully what I mean when I urge people to escape adulthood. Why do we spend such large chunks of our time taking things so darn seriously? Or, more importantly, why don't we realize that the things we usually approach with so much solemnity are the exact wrong things?

I believe we should look at children as teachers— miniature "sherpas" guiding us to the life Erma Bombeck describes. Children are active, there's no doubt about that. But I've never seen a kid complain to another about how stressed she is. I've never seen a youngster answer the question, "How have you been?" with the proud reply, "Busy!" And I've never seen a tyke who's impressed by things hailed as "practical."

Children live life with reckless abandon. Sure, they're messy and loud and sometimes uncouth, but then again, they could care less what other people think of them. They'd burn the pink candle sculpted like a rose, and then try to figure out how to melt the plain and boring ones into something resembling a dinosaur. Kids love how it feels to drive down the road with the wind raking through their hair (and they laugh at the wild results when the ride is over). They collect grass stains like Boy Scouts collect badges—with honor. They laugh at a dog chasing its tail, and cry when a caterpillar gets killed by an errant soccer ball. Kids don't have regretful lists of things they wish they'd done differently.

In short, kids just get it. The thing that's easy to forget is that we all used to get it. (I've never met anyone who hasn't been a kid—at least once.) The cobwebs may be dense, and the rust caked on thick, but it's worth the effort to clean them off and relearn what we forgot.

When in doubt, consult a sherpa.

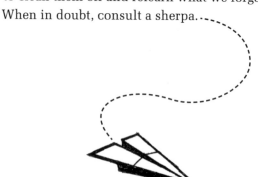

Acknowledgements

We'd like to thank all of the good people who have supported us through the years, including everyone who has hired us to share this message with their organization, purchased something from our store, given us advice, or just sent an encouraging e-mail or posted a nice comment on our blog. How fortunate we are that there are way too many to count. Your support and enthusiasm has been gold, Jerry, gold! A special note of thanks goes to our awesome editor, Pat, along with Jenna, Sue, Doug, and our unflinchingly supportive parents. And to Lucy Ruth, our beautiful little girl, we love you more every day.

About the Authors

It all started out as a pretty simple love story. Jason Kotecki first drew his lovable cartoon characters for his girlfriend Kim sometime before the turn of the century. The couple shared a kindred childlike spirit, and Jason used the drawings, which represented the couple as children, on many homemade (aka cheap) gifts designed to win her heart. Luckily for him, this downright sappy ploy helped him to not only win her heart, but also her hand in marriage. The characters took on lives of their own and in 2000, the real Kim and Jason decided to build a company to share the comic strip and its inspiring message. It has been a wild ride ever since. They have written books, created a weekly TV show, and criss-crossed the country sharing their belief that a life that embraces a childlike spirit is a life that is less stressful and way more fun.

Visit **www.KimandJason.com** to find more books written by Kim & Jason and to learn more about bringing them in to speak to your organization!

Is there an adult in YOUR soup?